BOUNCING BACK

AND COPING WITH CHANGE

Building Emotional & Social Resilience in

Young People Aged 9-14

Tina Rae

Tina Rae

BOUNCING BACK
AND COPING
WITH CHANGE

*Building Emotional &
Social Resilience in
Young People Aged 9-14*

HINTON HOUSE Emotional Literacy Resources

HINTONHOUSE

First published in 2016 by
Hinton House Publishers Ltd, Newman House, 4 High Street, Buckingham, MK18 1NT, UK
T +44 (0)1280 822557 F +44 (0) 560 3135274 E info@hintonpublishers.com
www.hintonpublishers.com

British Library Cataloguing in Publication Data
A CIP catalogue record for this book is available from the British Library.

ISBN 978 1 906531 68 3
Printed and bound in the United Kingdom

Contents

Acknowledgements

My thanks go to Sarah Miles at Hinton House Publishers.

About the Author

Dr Tina Rae has more thirty years' experience working with children, adults and families in both clinical and educational contexts within local authorities and specialist educational services. She currently works as a Consultant Educational and Child Psychologist in a range of SEBD/SEMH and mainstream contexts and for Compass Fostering as a consultant Psychologist supporting foster carers, social workers and looked-after children. She is an Academic and Professional tutor for the Doctorate in Educational and Child Psychology at the University of East London. She is a registered member of the Health and Care Professions Council, a full member of the British Psychological Society and a member of the editorial board for the SEBDA journal *Emotional and Behavioural Difficulties* and for the *International Journal of Nurture in Education*. Tina is also a member of SEBDA, a member of ENSEC (European Network for Social and Emotional Competence) and, until recently, a trustee of the Nurture Group Network (NGN).

Tina has published more than 75 titles on topics including well-being, attachment, emotional literacy, behavioural problems, anger and stress management, critical incidents, cognitive behavioural therapy, motivational interviewing, solution focused brief therapy, loss and bereavement in young people, youth offending and social skills development.

Her current research is into staff well-being and resilience including peer group supervision systems.

Tina is a regular speaker at both national and international conferences and events, and also provides training courses and supervision for school-based staff in both special and mainstream contexts and Educational Psychology services across the UK and internationally.

tinarae@hotmail.co.uk
t.m.rae@uel.ac.uk

Preface

Building resilience in order to promote and maintain well-being is clearly an essential objective for all of us who work with children and young people and who support their emotional well-being, both within and outside of the learning context.

Despite risk and challenge factors, many children and young people can and do overcome adversity. For those who present as more vulnerable, there is clearly hope in the fact that these coping skills can be taught and learnt and that negative patterns of thinking, feeling and behaving can be changed and more positive alternatives can be provided. These are life-long skills which all of us – adults and young people – need to work at and develop on a continual basis throughout our lives.

Positive psychology offers us all hope for a more resilient future and I sincerely believe that this publication will prompt those who care for and nurture young people to continue to focus on developing their own skills and approaches to supporting the well-being of those young people at the individual, group and systems levels.

These twenty sessions cannot possibly provide staff with all of the resources to meet all these objectives. However, I do feel that they can be used to provide support for individual children and groups of young people in terms of developing their resilience and engagement in the happy habits of positive thinking. Ultimately, the sessions can and should support the development of their well-being, whilst also prompting staff and carers to consider changes to the school and home context, which may reinforce and develop resilience and more positive thinking, feeling and behavioural patterns on a daily basis.

Tina Rae
2016

Introduction

In today's complex and often challenging social and learning environments, we know that there is an increasing need to promote resilience in children and young people – particularly in those who are more vulnerable due to a range of risk factors in their lives. That is, the ability to bounce back when things have gone wrong and to keep going and persist even in the face of adversity. The importance of creating a resilient staff team and a whole-school approach based on the philosophy and approaches emanating from Positive Psychology is also a key objective for all of us who work with children and young people.

These practical activities and exercises aim to support teaching staff and carers in meeting these objectives, making use of a range of key tools and strategies from evidence-based approaches such as mindfulness, solution-focused brief therapy and cognitive behavioural therapy.

These are the tools that enable children and young people to develop the resilience they will need to cope with the challenges of life in both the learning and social context. The pressures that they currently face in terms of social media, early sexualisation, school work, friendship and relationship issues and sometimes of financial uncertainty can all seem overwhelming – particularly if these are compounded by additional vulnerability factors or early childhood trauma. The identification of protective factors therefore becomes paramount, as does access to programmes of support which facilitate the development of resilience. This requires the development of a positive and outward looking mindset in which negative thinking and patterns of behaviour are challenged and altered, as well as enhancing the ability to engage in daily happy habits that reinforce strengths and maintain and further build well-being.

It is hoped that these twenty structured sessions will provide the resources, strategies and tools to build such resilience in children and young people, whilst also prompting those who care for them to reflect upon their own strategies and the systems they have in place for promoting and maintaining their own well-being and creating a resilience-promoting social and learning context for those they care for and nurture.

Emotional & Mental Well-being

The Department of Education and the Mental Health Foundation (www.mentalhealth.org.uk) define a mentally healthy child as one who can:

- Develop psychologically, emotionally, intellectually and spiritually
- Initiate, develop and sustain mutually satisfying personal relationships
- Use and enjoy solitude

- Become aware of others and empathise with them
- Play and learn
- Develop a sense of right and wrong
- Face problems and setbacks and learn from them

This list is further built upon by Helpguide (www.helpguide.org) to include a sense of well-being and contentment, a zest for living, resilience (the ability to 'bounce back') and creative as well as intellectual development.

On initial reading, this list may appear somewhat simplistic. However, once we begin to reflect upon our own lives and relate these descriptors to young people in schools, it is possible to see how it can provide an initial starting point for identifying problems and difficulties. As Prever states in his book *Mental Health in Schools* (2006), 'They are useful indicators when we consider their opposites – an activity that way gives us some insight into the meaning of mental health problems and mental illness.' (p.10).

Raising Awareness

The Office for National Statistics (2003) noted that over 10% of children aged between 5 and 15 years are affected by a mental health problem and that this figure rises to 11.2% for students of statutory secondary school age. This means that the average secondary school of 1,000 pupils will have:

- 50 students with depression
- 10 affected by eating disorders
- 100 suffering/experiencing 'significant distress'
- 10-20 students with obsessive compulsive disorder
- 5-10 attempting suicide

Recent statistics from the Young Minds website further illustrate the increasing concerns of those of us who support and care for young people today:

- 1 in 10 children and young people aged 5 - 16 suffer from a diagnosable mental health disorder - that is around three children in every class
- Between 1 in every 12 and 1 in 15 children and young people deliberately self-harm
- There has been a big increase in the number of young people being admitted to hospital because of self-harm. Over the last ten years this figure has increased by 68%
- More than half of all adults with mental health problems were diagnosed in childhood. Less than half were treated appropriately at the time
- Nearly 80,000 children and young people suffer from severe depression
- Over 8,000 children aged under 10 years old suffer from severe depression

Introduction

- 72% of children in care have behavioural or emotional problems - these are some of the most vulnerable people in our society 95% of imprisoned young offenders have a mental health disorder. Many of them are struggling with more than one disorder

- The number of young people aged 15-16 with depression nearly doubled between the 1980s and the 2000s

- The proportion of young people aged 15-16 with a conduct disorder more than doubled between 1974 and 1999

(Young Minds website 2015)

As Prever suggests, 'This, then, is the task faced by schools. Wherever possible, we need to find ways to prevent these problems in young people from developing. We need to act early with our own school-based support systems and refer on to – and work directly with – mental health professionals where this is felt necessary and desirable.' (2006, p.13)

Teachers and those who work with young people in schools can and do successfully prevent the escalation of mental health problems in their students by understanding more about protective factors and ensuring that they are promoted at the individual, group and system level across the whole-school community. This, in turn, can then support systems and approaches at both individual and group levels to build resilience and overall well-being.

Resilience

What is Resilience?

Resilience is about 'bouncing back' from what life throws at us. It is about being strong inside and able to adapt well to changes and difficulties. It is about flourishing in life, despite our circumstances.

If young people are resilient they will be able to cope better with problems, they will have better health and they will be happier and more fulfilled. They will also be less likely to develop emotional problems like depression or anxiety.

But resilience is not just something you have or don't have. The important truth is that we can help all children to become more resilient. We can't protect children from all the things that may cause them distress throughout their lives. But we can help children become more resilient so that they are more able to cope with life's uncertainties and problems. And all children, no matter what their background, will have to face problems and changes in their lives. So our support is really important in helping children become more resilient.

> *It is not the strongest of the species that survives, nor the most intelligent.*
> *It is the one that is the most adaptable to change.*
>
> – Charles Darwin

Coping with Change

The way in which young children and indeed adults cope with change is one important component of our mental health. This capacity tends to be shaped by our own unique combination of nature, nurture and events, and a resulting balance in our lives between both risk and resilience. For many young people who have experienced secure attachments and nurturing in their early years, adults will be seen as trustworthy and reliable. These are the people whom children can go to when they are attempting to deal with difficult issues, uncomfortable feelings and thoughts, and times of transition such as secondary school transfer. For those whose experiences of adults are more chaotic and whose relationships did not lead to the development of resilience, trusting adults and regulating their strong feelings may be slightly more problematic. Children who are more vulnerable will tend to find it more difficult to ask for help, and also to cope with any underlying anxieties which they experience during the process of change.

Resilience

Risk Factors

It is important to highlight the fact that risk does not cause mental health problems in children and young people; however, it is something that is cumulative and can predispose children and young people to poor outcomes in the longer term. It is therefore essential that those who are working with young children, both in the learning and social contexts, aim to minimise the number and extent of risks that they are exposed to. It is not always possible to remove the risk itself but an awareness of the presence of risk can quite often change the way that adults understand a young person's needs and respond to them. It is vital at the outset that school-based staff, for example, have access to information which would ensure the identification of any potential risk factors or existing risk factors for individual children and young people. These can include the following:

- Genetic influences
- Learning difficulties
- Specific development delay
- Communication difficulties
- A difficult temperament
- Physical illness
- Previous academic failure
- Low levels of self-esteem

Predisposing factors within families can also include the following:

- Overt parental conflict
- Family breakdown
- Inconsistent or unclear discipline in the home
- Hostile and rejecting relationships
- Failure to adapt to the child's development needs
- Physical/sexual abuse and/or neglect or emotional neglect
- Parental psychiatric illness
- Parental criminality, alcoholism, drug abuse and personality disorder
- Death and loss including the loss of friendships

Predisposing factors in the wider community can include the following:

- Socio-economic disadvantage
- Homelessness
- Disaster, accidents, war and other overwhelming events
- Discrimination
- Other significant life events

Promoting Resilience

It is vital for the emotional well-being of children and young people that school-based staff engage in the process of promoting resilience in all Key Stages and particularly upon the stage of transition between Key Stage 2 and 3.

Newman (2002) defined a resilient child as one who 'can resist adversity, cope with uncertainty and recover more successfully from traumatic events or episodes'. He described resilience as being a set of skills that are acquired through experience, although there may of course be some inherited aspects. Resilience is not about invulnerability but is essentially about our capacity to cope. Continuous and extreme adversity is likely to drain even the most resilient children and adults. Rutter (1985, 1987) argued that resilience is created when risk is reduced through a series of protective mechanisms or factors; it is these that can change a child's trajectory in life. When young people are supported in developing a positive appraisal of themselves and the ability to think differently or in a more solution-focused way about events, they are then able to feel differently about their own competence. In essence they believe in their own ability to cope. Rutter also argued that risk is reduced when the exposure to risk is altered in some way. Rutter highlights the following factors which protect young people in adversity:

- The ability to integrate experiences into their belief systems
- The presence of self-esteem
- The ability to be proactive in relation to ongoing stress
- Having secure, affectional relationships
- Some measure of success and achievement
- Interaction with others in securing gains
- Parental modelling or redeeming relationships in other words, modelling by another supportive adult
- The ability to process events and experiences in a meaningful way
- Gaining mastery over stressful events

Daniel & Wassell (2002) developed the notion of domains of resilience. They highlighted six areas of a young person's life where resilience could be promoted. These are as follows:

- Secure base
- Education
- Friendships
- Talents and interests
- Positive values
- Social competence

The idea of such 'resilient strings' is similar to Rutter's concept of protective mechanisms. These are processes which interact with each other over time in order to reinforce the level of resilience a child or young person actually has. It is also likely that in resilient children one domain of resilience will positively impact on another. For example, a young child who has a musical talent and who is asked to perform in a school band or choir is also likely to develop friendships and as a result will take up a higher profile social role in the school which is more valued. This in turn will promote his or her educational outcomes in the long run.

Resilience in Young People

Research has consistently identified the following factors as being protective of a young person's well-being and mental health:

- Being female (in younger children)
- Having a secure attachment experience
- Showing an outgoing temperament as an infant
- Having good communication skills and sociability
- Being a planner and having a belief in control
- Humour
- Good problem-solving skills and a positive attitude
- Experiences of success and achievement
- Faith or spirituality
- Having the capacity to reflect
- Having at least one good parent/carer–child relationship or a supportive adult
- Affection
- Clear, consistent discipline
- Support for education
- Supportive long-term relationships or the absence of severe discord
- Wider support networks
- Good housing
- High standard of living
- High morale at school with positive policies for behaviour, attitudes and anti-bullying
- Opportunities for valued social roles
- Range of sport and leisure activities

Building Resilience

As discussed above, resilient children are those who can resist adversity, cope with uncertainty and recover more successfully from traumatic events or episodes. Psychologists have long recognised that some children develop well despite growing up in high risk environments. This capacity to cope with adversity and to even be strengthened by it is at the heart of resilience. It is not something that people either have or don't have; resilience is learnable and teachable and as we learn we can increase the range of strategies available to us when things get difficult. In effect the theory of resilience provides us with an optimistic message of hope. It is indeed possible to learn resilient thinking patterns and skills which in turn help us to become more accurate and flexible in our thinking. Children can begin to do this at a much earlier age than previously thought and it is vital that they do so, given that stress and adversity are an inevitable part of our lives. It therefore makes good sense, as MacConville (2011, p.19) suggests, to teach children and young people how to:

- Have an optimistic bias
- Challenge their negative thinking patterns
- Think outside the box
- Bounce back from adversity

Children need to become resilient to overcome the many adversities they face and will face in life: they cannot do it alone. They need adults who know how to promote resilience and who are, indeed, becoming more resilient themselves.

Seven Learnable Skills of Resilience

Karen Reivich (2002) and her colleagues at Penn University identified seven abilities that characterise resilient individuals. These are presented in the chart below:

Emotional awareness or regulation	Ability to identify what you are feeling and manage these feelings appropriately
Impulse control	Ability to tolerate ambiguity and not rush decision-making
Optimism	Optimistic explanatory style – wed to reality
Causal analysis	Ability to view difficulties from a number of perspectives, and consider many factors
Empathy	Ability to read and understand emotions of others. Helps build relationships with others and gives social support
Self-efficacy	Confidence in your ability to solve problems – involves knowing your strengths and weaknesses
Reaching out	Being prepared to take appropriate risk – a willingness to try things and view failure as part of life

Overall, Reivich highlights the fact that resilience is not an 'either/or' trait, rather it is a continuum and all of us are to some extent able to increase our ability to rise to the challenges and setbacks that life presents us with. It is therefore important that any supportive mechanisms used to facilitate change and encourage children to manage a smooth transition include the development of resilience-building skills. Children need to be taught these strategies and given copious opportunities to practise them on a regular basis. These kinds of 'happy habits' of positive psychology are essentially life skills which will ensure that resilience is continually reinforced throughout the young person's time at school and beyond.

Developing Resilience

The Whole-School Approach

It is important to highlight that there are practical aspects of the school environment that can and do have a positive impact upon the development of resilience. Whole-school, approaches which promote resilience and a smooth transition, also ensure consistency and coherence across each of the components. It is important that policy documents are written and produced, but also that these are seen to be implemented: in other words, the policy is modelled in practice for all members of the school community. The following examples provide an idea of some whole-school approaches that ensure the promotion of resilience in the change process and the daily lives of children and young people.

A school culture and ethos characterised by:

- Every child being a respected, safe learner
- Mistakes being allowed
- All staff knowing children well
- A shared school vision
- Incorporating restorative approaches – a focus on understanding, not blame; a focus on solutions
- Continuous improvement – review and learn
- Communication for all
- Valuing the whole child
- Teamwork
- Empowering pupils, preparing young people to be independent
- Listening
- Consistent approaches to young people with difficulties
- Shared information
- Being flexible and approachable
- Fun
- Role-modelling
- A consistency of whole-school approach
- All staff feeling valued and included
- Valuing the contribution of all children
- Children feeling secure and that they belong

Developing Resilience

- Having a house system, house points, celebrations and sense of belonging
- Having an ethos based on faith

A school leadership that models and enables:

- A clear purpose for the school that is consistently articulated and shared with staff, children and parents
- All members of the school community to understand their role and to take up that role
- A willingness to learn and to change
- Mistakes to be made and learned from
- Fairness
- Consultation

Curriculum

- A differentiated curriculum – giving a chance for all to succeed – adapted for specific groups of pupils and taught in small groups where appropriate
- Social and Emotional Aspects of Learning (SEAL) embedded in the practice and culture of the school
- Personal, Social, Health and Economic Education (PSHE); for whole school, groups and individuals
- Ownership (negotiated) of Individual Education Plans (IEPs) and Individual Behaviour Plans (IBP) targets
- 'Opening Minds' – cross-curriculum approach linking work to real life issues and topics across subjects
- Personalised, Alternative, Curriculum Experience (PACE) – 11 hours per week with the same space, teachers and peers
- Planning for sensory curriculum to meet the needs of the pupils with profound and complex difficulties
- Promoting Alternative Thinking Strategies (PATHS)
- Themed weeks, for example, diversity week

Teaching & learning

- Teach emotional literacy
- Shared responsibility
- Rights
- Respect
- Educational visits, trips and journeys
- Keep the same teaching assistants with class groups throughout their school lives with classes throughout school

- Structured, displayed timetables in each class
- All pupils are greeted warmly

Policies

- Open-door policy for parents
- Consistent policies across the school
- Whole-school agreements
- Clear inclusion policies
- Clear, consistent policies on anti-bullying
- Clear boundaries and guidelines
- Whole-school development of behaviour policy
- Consistent marking policy
- Transitions policy for Key Stage 1 to Key Stage 2 and KS2 to KS3

Pupil participation

- Peer mentoring
- Students contribute to annual reviews and target setting
- School council
- Students involved in decision-making

Assessing, recording, celebrating achievement

- Celebrating all achievement – academic, music, sports, drama, arts
- Noticeboard 'about our school'
- Celebration assemblies
- Celebration weeks: books, creative, science, etc.
- Weekly 'rejoice' assemblies
- Rewards evenings
- Rewards scheme
- Achievement medals including 'kindness' medal

Pupil support services

- Social skills groups (talking partners, circle of friends)
- Lunchtime play scheme
- 'Talk About' secondary school self-esteem nurture programme for individuals
- Small group support
- Pastoral system/support workers
- Family support workers

Developing Resilience

- Named 'key person' for each child
- Buddy scheme – peer mentoring
- Counsellor on site each week
- A two week summer school programme for Year 7
- Music therapy
- A safe place for pupils to go for time out – always staffed
- Nurture room offering cooking, circle time, games, etc.
- Variety of before- and after-school clubs, including a breakfast club

Working with external agencies (in-reach and out-reach)

- Family support workers
- Behaviour support team
- Well-researched work experience placements
- Music therapy via occupational therapist
- External training providers
- Good multi-professional meetings and shared information
- Speech and language therapy
- Educational psychology

Parent/carer partnerships

- Children's Centre links to support families and school
- Regular meetings
- Letters
- Home/school books
- Parent training opportunities in the school
- Parent inclusion in weekly assemblies, performances, volunteering in school
- Being transparent with parents and children, for example holding end of year meetings with parents to discuss reports and targets

Staff mental health & well-being

- Training – developing staff understanding of mental health
- Skills audits and in-house training
- Staff support group
- Performance management process
- Social events
- Approachable senior staff

Why is Resilience Important?

The Need to Develop Resilience & Resilient Relationships

Any approach to identifying and then supporting the less resilient or more at risk young people in the school context also needs to incorporate a focus on building and developing the resilience of both carers and the young person themselves. In order to provide a sense of trust, feelings of self-worth and reliability in young people, caregivers must be able to work together with the young person and build a positive and resilient relationship. We know that traumatised young people can present as hostile, rejecting and powerful individuals. Carers must therefore be able to establish and maintain firm and consistent boundaries, and also be skilled at negotiating within these boundaries, as well as being creative in designing situations whereby the young person can make positive choices for themselves and learn to be assertive in an appropriate way. We know that this will build a young person's emotional resilience.

In order to be successful carers, adults need to have their own strong and well-developed emotional resilience and to have successfully dealt with losses and traumas in their own lives.

> *Adults who intend to provide a child with a sense of psychological safely that is sufficient to resolve and integrate experiences associated with trauma and loss, need to have resolved any similar experiences in their own attachment histories in order to remain present for the child affectively and cognitively whenever the memory of those experiences emerge. (Hughes, 2003, p.273)*

They also need to enjoy working in cooperation, within structured settings and have a range of approaches to adopt in order to achieve compromise. Each individual caregiver requires the capacity and ability to self-reflect and to possess a good understanding and acceptance of themselves as an individual.

Resilience theory has been further influenced in recent years by psychologists working within the field of Positive Psychology, who adopt the position that all aspects of life need to be embraced and that coping with risk and challenge are actually good for us. Stress and adversity are something that we will all experience and it is therefore essential that children learn how to manage such challenges. As Carol Craig, Chief Executive of the Centre for Confidence and Well-being in Glasgow, writes, 'even with the best care, for children and young people the world can be full of adversity' (2007, p.92).

Promoting resilience and the positive sense of self and coping skills that result are clearly an essential within both the social and learning contexts for all young people and consequently should be the key and essential elements of any intervention or approach both within and out of the school context.

The Role of Education

An essential starting point in any approach to building resilience and resilient relationships is the notion that all children and young people need to experience positive acceptance, regardless of the behaviours displayed and particularly when these are extremely challenging.

This is in keeping with Parental Acceptance-Rejection Theory (PA-RT) (Rohner, 2004), which highlights the need for carers to communicate acceptance to young people and also identify culturally appropriate ways of avoiding behaviours that might indicate parental coldness and a lack of affection towards the young person. The ways in which a caregiver thinks and feels about a child's behaviours will determine his or her parenting behaviours. Parenting behaviours convey certain messages to the child. The child's thinking and feeling will be affected by those messages and there will be a consequent impact on his/her behaviour and development.

The parenting cycle encompasses the range of daily interactions of family life from the smallest of interactions to major emotional and behavioural difficulties. Each interaction between the caregiver and the young person has an incremental effect on that young person and this impacts on:

- Their self-belief

- Their beliefs about other people

Both of these have an influence on the young person's functioning and development. Adults also need to understand and recognise their own thoughts and feelings and how this impacts on them as carers. Making use of the tools provided by *Cognitive Behavioural Approach* (Rae & Egan, 2009), *Motivational Interview Approach* (Rae & Smith, 2009) and *Solution Focused Approach* (Rae & Smith, 2009) to further enhance such an awareness and to develop skills of self-reflection might form another essential part of any approach.

Overall, it is seen as essential that a carer's well-being is maintained and that their level of resilience is further developed and supported by appropriate support frameworks, including peer supervision and carer support groups.

The Role of Positive Psychology

Such a strength-based approach is entirely consistent with the key aims of Positive Psychology. It moves away from the within-child deficit model to a model based upon building capacity and strength.

The goal of Positive Psychology is essentially to enhance human strengths such as optimism, courage, honesty, self-understanding and interpersonal skills. This is the opposite of what Dr Martin Seligman calls 'focusing on the broken things and on repairing the damage of past traumas' (2008). Positive Psychology provides a means of helping the individual to use their inner resources as a buffer against setbacks and adversity in life. Developing such skills helps to prevent individuals from becoming depressed. As Seligman states, 'it's not about how to heal; it's about to have a great life' (p.68). Seligman and his associates developed an intervention designed to instil a sense of optimism, which they defined as a positive way of construing the failures and setbacks that normally occur in life.

This is similar to approaches utilised in Cognitive Behavioural Therapy (CBT), in which participants are encouraged to construe failures in a more positive light. For example, if you consider that failures are stable and pervasive then they will last forever and subsequently undermine everything that you try to do - this will ultimately lead to depression. However, if we can train young people and ourselves to view such setbacks and difficulties as temporary or affecting only a small part of our lives then the depression can be averted.

This is clearly a key objective of our work with vulnerable young people, which focuses upon ensuring that they have optimum opportunities to experience positive emotions. This will ensure their ability to attend to school work, increase working memory and verbal fluency and also ensure an increased openness to information.

Seligman highlights three essential areas that are key to happiness and well-being. These are:
- Hope and optimism
- Flow
- Happy memories

All three of these can be seen to improve learning and levels of resilience both within and outside of the classroom.

Hope & Optimism

Building hope and optimism is clearly a key aspect of education. Young people will generally learn better if they feel hopeful about their own skills and their future lives and it is optimism which ensures that both young people and adults can develop resiliency skills: bouncing back from adversity and remaining in control of their own emotions and behaviours. As noted above, resilience is something that develops through positive relationships and it is vital, according to positive psychologists, that young people have the opportunity to develop these traits in living what is termed a 'connected childhood'. This involves having at least one adult who believes totally in their worth and abilities and who also has the capacity and commitment to redirect the student towards being productive, successful and happy.

The Concept of Flow

Key to promoting and maintaining this optimism is the concept of flow. This is defined as a sense of deep engagement in an activity during which time passes extremely quickly and the individual is able to work at full capacity. Nothing distracts them as they learn and make progress towards their ultimate goals. The aftermath of this state is truly invigorating as the individual will feel happy and relaxed with a sense of achievement. This is something that we should strive for with all our children and young people. However, translating this kind of absorption into more formal learning settings can be difficult in that it is easier to achieve flow in activities which are self-selected and intrinsically enjoyable. What is essential is that the challenge is relevant to the task. If the challenge is too great for the child then they will feel anxious or frustrated, whereas when the challenge is appropriate there is a good balance between the required skill and the young person's ability, ensuring that they will succeed and begin to achieve this state of flow.

Happy Memories

Happy memories are 'extremely important for ensuring happiness and well-being; the way that we feel about the past and our experiences can clearly impact both positively and negatively on how we feel and function at the present time' (Seligman, 2008, p.12). Students who only remember how badly they performed last time they did a task are likely to underperform the next time – this is basic common sense. What carers and teachers need to do is to encourage students to pay attention to what they did well and what they got right, particularly when struggling with new challenges.

For this reason many psychologists will advocate the use of a five-step cycle for developing resilience and well-being. This was originated by Hallowell (2002). This cycle is something that continues throughout our lives and, although it is described in five distinct stages, in reality these all blend into a smooth circular process. Each of the five steps leads logically to the next and when they are working successfully for an individual they promote overall psychological well-being. This includes emotional strength, physical health, moral behaviour and optimism. The five steps are as follows:

- Step 1 Connect
- Step 2 Play
- Step 3 Practise
- Step 4 Master
- Step 5 Recognse

The diagram on p.19 provides a more detailed explanation of each stage.

This kind of approach is particularly useful for carers and teachers in terms of recognising the value and importance of Positive Psychology both in the learning and social context. Children and young people need not only to master academic tasks but also to master the emotional aspects and challenges of living in an increasingly complex world. Being able to manage stress and 'bounce back' from adversity are clearly essentials.

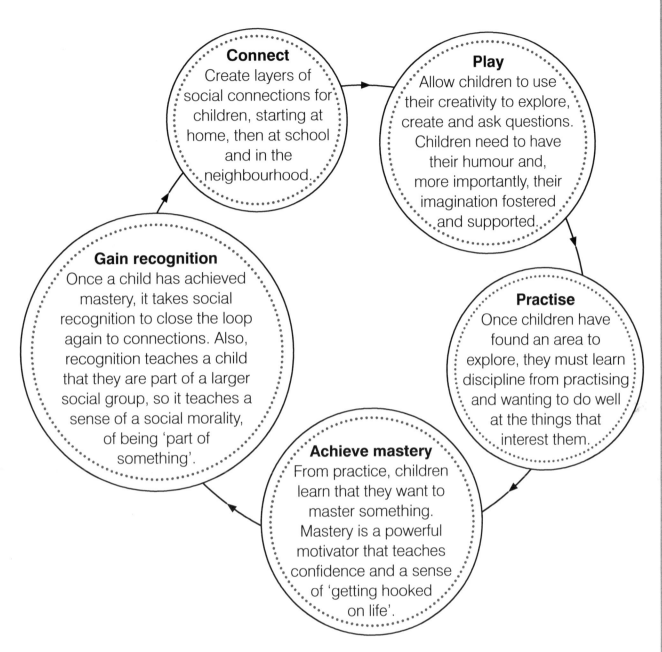

Connect
Create layers of social connections for children, starting at home, then at school and in the neighbourhood.

Play
Allow children to use their creativity to explore, create and ask questions. Children need to have their humour and, more importantly, their imagination fostered and supported.

Gain recognition
Once a child has achieved mastery, it takes social recognition to close the loop again to connections. Also, recognition teaches a child that they are part of a larger social group, so it teaches a sense of a social morality, of being 'part of something'.

Practise
Once children have found an area to explore, they must learn discipline from practising and wanting to do well at the things that interest them.

Achieve mastery
From practice, children learn that they want to master something. Mastery is a powerful motivator that teaches confidence and a sense of 'getting hooked on life'.

Managing Stress & Negative Thinking

According to Cox (1981) the effects of stress may be subjective (aggression, fatigue, low self-esteem), behavioural (restlessness, emotional outbursts, taking drugs), cognitive (inability to concentrate, mental blocks, hypersensitive) and physiological (sweating, dry mouth, increased heart rate). A useful definition is provided by Dunham (1992) who states that 'stress is a process of behavioural, emotional, mental and physical reactions caused by prolonged, increasing or new pressures which are significantly greater than coping resources' (p.3). It is such coping resources that young people need to make use of in learning, studying and examination and social contexts.

However, it is important to emphasise the fact that coping is also a complex and multi-dimensional process in which the individual aims to make 'cognitive and behavioural efforts to manage specific external and internal demands that are appraised as taxing or exceeding the resources of the person. These cognitive and behavioural efforts are constantly changing as a function of continuous appraisal and reappraisal of the person-environment relationship which is also always changing' (Dunham, 1992, p.210). This definition is enriched by Frydenberg (1997) who also incorporates Bandura's (1977) concept of self-efficacy into her definition. Overall, it appears to be the individual's perception of the situation that is central to the coping employed.

Frydenberg (1997) states that 'people who believe they can exercise control do not engage in apprehensive thinking, they are not bothered by threat or challenge' (p.27). This is echoed by Roskies & Lazarus (1980) who write, 'it is not enough to possess the skills of competent coping; one must believe one has them' (p.57). It could be argued that this belief will be enhanced through the teaching of coping skills. You are more likely to believe that you have these skills if you are or have been actively engaged in the learning and practising of them. Any programme of support therefore needs to support carers in providing young people with copious opportunities to learn and practise a range of effective stress management skills (Rae, 2010) in order to cope more effectively with the stressors associated with everyday life in the real world.

Using Cognitive Behavioural Therapy (CBT)

Cognitive Behavioural Therapy

CBT reveals the role that thoughts play in relation to both our emotions and our behaviours and advocates that changes in thought processes can have a significant effect upon altering behaviours. Unlike many 'talking treatments' that traditional therapists use, CBT focuses upon the 'here and now', as well as ways of improving the individual's state of mind in the present time. This is innovative in the sense that there is no focus on the causes of distress or past symptoms as there is with traditional psychotherapy.

Restructuring Thought Processes

Young people are frequently flooded with anxious and negative thoughts and doubts. These messages will often reinforce a state of inadequacy and/or low levels of self- esteem. The process of CBT helps to support young people in reconsidering these negative assumptions. It also allows them to learn how to change their self-perceptions in order to improve their mental and emotional state - this is the key aim of this kind of intervention. Changing negative thought patterns or opinions will ultimately help young people to become more able to control and change their behaviours, but this does take practice. This is why, as with anger management interventions, another key element of the approach is the requirement to learn, and to put into practice, the skills or strategies discussed in any session.

The ABC of Cognitive Behavioural Therapy

The CBT approach breaks a particular problem into three smaller parts:
- **A:** the **activating event**, this is often referred to as the 'trigger' — the thing that causes you to engage in the negative thinking.
- **B:** represents these negative **beliefs**, which can include thoughts, rules and demands, and the meanings the individual attaches to both external and internal events.
- **C:** the **consequences**, or emotions, and the behaviours and physical sensations accompanying these different emotions. It is important to highlight and discuss with young people how the way that they think about a problem can affect how they feel physically and emotionally. It can also alter what they do about it. This is why the key aim for CBT is to break the negative, vicious cycle that some young people may find themselves in. For example, if you think that you will get your work wrong you feel angry, and then you do not give it a try in case it is wrong.

Using Cognitive Behavioural Therapy (CBT)

Core Beliefs

Core beliefs are the strong, enduring ideas that we may have about ourselves. This kind of belief system gives rise to rules, demands or assumptions which in turn produce automatic thoughts. Core beliefs generally fall into three main categories: beliefs about yourself; beliefs about other people in the world; beliefs that are either positive or negative. What is important is to identify our core beliefs and to also consider why these may or may not be unhelpful. In this way we can begin to identify negative automatic thoughts (NATs). Some of these thoughts that students may hold about themselves could include the following:

- I always look ugly.

- I don't understand this work.

- He thinks I'm stupid and an idiot.

- She gave me a nasty look.

- I'm just such a useless person.

- I can't do that and I'll never be able to do it like other people can.

When working with students in identifying such faulty thinking, the main aim is to encourage them to break the negative cycle. These NATs can arise from a number of errors in our thinking, including the following six types of faulty thinking:

(1) DOING DOWN!

- Only focusing on negatives.

- Only seeing the bad bit in something that was good overall.

- Not counting a positive, e.g.: 'He only wants to go out with me because he can't find anyone else.'

(2) BLOWING UP OUT OF PROPORTION!

- Making things worse than they are.

- It's all or nothing, e.g.: 'I only got 78% and not 100% – it's not good enough!'

- Magnifying the problem, e.g.: 'I got the answer wrong and everyone in the class laughed at me! It's a catastrophe! I'll never get over it!'

(3) PREDICTING FAILURE!

- Mind-reading to predict failure, e.g.: 'I bet they are all laughing at me! I know he hates me!'

- Fortune-telling – knowing you will fail, e.g.: 'I know I won't be able to do that work/I know they won't like me.'

(4) OVER-EMOTIONAL THOUGHTS!

- With this faulty thinking our emotions become very strong and cloud the way we think and understand things.

- Because we feel bad we presume everything is bad – the emotions take over!

- We attach negative labels to ourselves, e.g.: I'm rubbish, stupid, a loser.

(5) SETTING YOURSELF UP!

- Setting targets too high and setting ourselves up to fail.

- I should, I must, I can't, I want, I shouldn't, etc.

- Creating an impossible standard to achieve.

(6) BLAME YOURSELF

- Everything that goes wrong/is wrong is our fault – even stuff we have no control over, e.g.: I got into my car and it broke down! I turned on the computer and it crashed!

When working with young people, it is important to allow them time to consider the effects that these NATs can have, prior to them beginning to implement some changes.

Case Study
Teaching Sam Coping Skills via a Group (CBT) Intervention

Sam presented as a teenage girl with low self-esteem and anxiety problems. She was particularly negative about her academic performance at school and held the core belief that she was thick and stupid – particularly at maths – and consequently, that it was a waste of time to even try new things. She thought she would fail, felt down and stupid and therefore gave up at the first hurdle or point at which a concept proved too difficult to understand or absorb. Breaking this negative cycle formed the main part of an initial one-to-one session and subsequent group sessions.

One of the most helpful interventions for developing new and more positive belief systems, and for challenging these negative automatic thoughts, is to test the evidence. Sam was therefore encouraged to engage in the following questioning process:

1. What is the evidence for this thought?
2. What is the evidence against this thought?
3. What would my best friend say if they heard my thought?
4. What would my teacher say if he heard my thought?
5. What would my parents or carers say if they heard my thought?
6. What would I say to my best friend if s/he had this same thought?
7. Am I making mistakes? For example, blowing things up out of proportion, forgetting my strengths or good points, self-blaming or predicting failure or thinking that I can mind-read what others are thinking?

This kind of strategy is particularly useful in terms of reinforcing the need to gather accurate evidence. What we believe about ourselves is not always true. It is not how others always see us and these kinds of beliefs need to be challenged in this way. Using this sort of questioning process, and gathering evidence in the form of such a behavioural experiment, is a particularly positive strategy for beginning to identify and challenge unhelpful beliefs that students may carry.

DAY & TIME	THOUGHT	Rate how much you believe it 1-10 (10=totally) (Use the THOUGHT SCALE)	EVIDENCE FOR the thought	EVIDENCE AGAINST the thought

Using Cognitive Behavioural Therapy (CBT)

THOUGHT	What would my best friend say to me?	What would I say to my best friend if they had this thought?	How much do I believe this thought now? 1-10 (10 = totally)

Reframing

Negative thoughts can be reframed into more positive, balanced and realistic ones through reframing. For example, 'I am just fat', could be reframed as 'I need to lose some weight and tone up a bit but my overall shape isn't that bad.' 'I always get the maths work wrong' could be reframed as 'Some of these sums are difficult but I know I can do the basics – I just need to work hard and find help in order to improve my skills.' This was the 'reframe' for Sam in the initial stages.

Distraction

Students can also be encouraged to control their thoughts by thinking of something else:

- They can describe in detail what they see around them in order to feel calmer. They can attempt to name all of their favourite bands.

- They can use self-talk techniques and repeat a positive coping message until the negative automatic thought has gone.

- They can 'bin' the thoughts by writing them down and then screwing them up and putting them into the bin – symbolically eradicating these negative thoughts.

- Students can keep a positive diary in order to record positive automatic thoughts (PATs) that may occur during the day, and also engage in realistic goal-setting which involves practice.

During the six-week group intervention, Sam was encouraged to make use of all the above strategies. Overall, what is important when students are engaged in learning and developing these skills is for adults to encourage them to set appropriate targets. Young people need to be reminded that we do not move forwards unless we set realistic goals for ourselves. These should be broken down into small, achievable steps and the ultimate goal continually focused upon. Setting targets allows us to visualise where we want to be in the future and if we feel that we have nowhere to go, or nothing to move towards, then ultimately we will not be able to effect the change necessary.

Incorporating Mindfulness Approaches

What is Mindfulness?

A key intervention which permeates the sessions is mindfulness. This is an approach which increases children's life skills by supporting them in developing the ability to both soothe and calm themselves; to pay attention to themselves in the world and to think about and reflect upon both their actions and their relationships. Clearly, such a set of 'happy habits' can only serve to further support overall well-being and more confident, optimistic and well-balanced young people.

At the outset it is important to point out the fact that mindfulness is not simply an abstract body of knowledge. It is, in essence, a practical set of skills. For human beings, daily living is often extremely stressful and busy. Mindfulness supports us in becoming more fully aware of living right now, in the present moment. There is an increasing body of research that shows that it can ultimately have long-term benefits for both our health and our levels of happiness.

Most of us, at some point, will have made a journey into work and then on arrival suddenly realised that we didn't actually remember engaging in the actual task of driving. There are also times when we may be lying in a bath or having a shower and feeling the warm water on our bodies but not actually being present in that moment. Very often we will be thinking about something that we have to do or an event that took place previously or a meeting that we might need to organise. For many of us we can become entrenched in living our lives on an almost automatic pilot. We barely live in the present and don't pay attention to what is happening in our lives currently at this particular moment. However, if we stop to really think about the situation it is this moment that is actually all that we have.

> 'Mindfulness is paying attention here and now with kindness and curiosity.'
> (Association for Mindfulness in Education)

Mindfulness has also been described as, 'The awareness that emerges through paying attention on purpose through the present moment, non-judgmentally, to the unfolding of experience moment by moment' (Kabat-Zinn, www.mindfulnet.org/page2.htm).

One of the easiest ways to get into a mindful state is to simply sit down on a chair, close your eyes and begin to focus on your breathing. As you sit still, relaxed but also alert, you can then direct your attention to the sensation of each inhalation and exhalation, and also become aware of the feeling of air as it enters and then leaves your mouth or nostrils. It is whilst doing this that other thoughts will enter into your mind. The idea is to become aware of such intrusions, noting each of these in turn without judgment and then simply letting

Incorporating Mindfulness Approaches

them pass. This is one of the key elements of mindfulness and the skill that is focused upon throughout the activities. Each of the sessions will incorporate an element of this practice whilst Session 13 provides a series of activities and encourages the students to begin a mindfulness diary and incorporate elements of practice into their daily lives both at home and at school.

The Benefits of Mindfulness

During the last 20 to 25 years there have been numerous studies which demonstrate that mindfulness provides benefits in a range of clinical settings, from pain and stress management through to management of depression. Work has also been highlighted in non-clinical groups (Baer, 2003; Greeson, 2009). Mindfulness training has at least five broad beneficial effects. It promotes:

- Increased sensory awareness

- Greater cognitive control

- Enhanced regulation of emotions

- Acceptance of transient thoughts and feelings

- The capacity to regulate attention

(Huppert & Johnson, 2010)

Sensory Awareness
Practising mindfulness nurtures the capacity to bring our sensory experience into our consciousness. This enables us to create the space to simply stop and just experience the moment in all its fullness. Being able to be in the moment and appreciate the positive sensory experiences that we have is not simply enjoyable, it also elicits positive emotions that feed into overall well-being, according to Barbara Frederickson of the University of North Carolina. In her research she has demonstrated that recurrently experiencing positive emotions simultaneously broadens our sensory awareness thus creating further opportunities for sensory savouring. This also builds psychological and emotional resilience overall (Fredrickson, 2009).

Cognitive Control
The goal of mindfulness is not to simply eliminate the mind of all thoughts and feelings but it is to anchor oneself to what one is currently experiencing in the sensory world. The idea is to allow thoughts to enter the mind quite freely and to simply note these in a non-judgmental and un-analytical manner. This is particularly useful in terms of managing busy minds, as mindfulness in effect promotes a de-centred perspective on these copious thoughts that we have. It enables us to create a distance between the thoughts that we have and our cognitive reactions to them. We can have a thought without actually having to act upon it. We can treat it just simply as a thought.

Emotional Regulation

It is very easy to become overwhelmed by intrusive emotional thoughts. These very often reflect uncomfortable situations which caused us to feel angry, embarrassed or stressed. Mindfulness encourages a more de-centred perspective on such feelings. Once again they should be noted and allowed to pass. If we just recognise the feelings, then we provide ourselves with the opportunity to choose how to respond to them rather than reacting automatically, engaging in patterns of automatic negative thinking which always tend to lead to this negative outcomes for the individual. If we recognise the feelings, then we provide ourselves with the opportunity to choose how to respond to them rather than reacting in an automatic fashion. This can prevent us from engaging in patterns of automatic negative thinking which always tend to lead the negative outcomes we do not really want for ourselves.

Acceptance

Treating our thoughts in this non-judgmental and more detached manner is also hugely positive in terms of accepting our thoughts and feelings. This is very important as it encourages us to be more tolerant and kind to ourselves. We do not need to beat ourselves up for having negative or intrusive thoughts or feelings; we simply have to accept them and know that we need to learn to be kinder to ourselves in both the short and longer terms.

Attention Regulation

Given the fact that mindfulness doesn't demand that we clear our minds of all thoughts and feelings but rather allow them to pass by and be noted, this in effect provides us with training in how to regulate and direct at will our attention. This is extremely important for young children in the learning context. Being able to bring back a wandering attention over and over again is, according to William James, 'the very route of judgment, character and will'. In his 1890 classic, *The Principles of Psychology*, James highlights the fact that education should improve this faculty and if it did so then it would be 'the education par excellence'.

The Evidence Base for Mindfulness in Schools

Historically, mindfulness has most often been used in a clinical context by practitioners aiming to support those suffering with stress, anxiety and depression. However, it has become increasingly apparent that using mindfulness as a preventative tool for children in schools offers a practical way forward.

There is, to a very great extent, an overlap with the current Social Emotional Aspects of Learning (SEAL) curriculum, specifically in the areas of developing self-awareness and emotional intelligence, motivation and social skills. As a tool used regularly and appropriately, mindfulness can increase children's level of self-awareness. It also nurtures their capacity to regulate automatic emotional reactions to events and difficulties that they may encounter on a daily basis in both school and social contexts. There is an increasing evidence base to support this intervention. This includes the publication in 2010 of the first peer-reviewed, controlled study on the delivery of mindfulness in schools. This was implemented by Huppert & Johnson from the Cambridge Well-Being Institute.

A four-week syllabus was delivered for use in independent, fee-paying schools, and in total 173 students were involved in the study. Mindfulness was taught during RE lessons, with each student being in one of 11 classes in the two schools. Six of those classes took normal RE lessons in order to provide a controlled group for the study, whilst the other five undertook mindfulness training. Initially the students were required to complete online questionnaires in order to assess their psychological well-being, resilience and reported levels of mindfulness. The measures used include the Warwick Edinburgh Mental Well-being Scale (NHS Health Scotland, 2006), the Ego Resiliency Scale (Block & Kremen, 1996) and the Cognitive Effective Mindfulness Scale (Feldman et al, 2007) revised.

Overall, it would seem that there was a significant increase in well-being amongst students who received the mindfulness intervention, but of most significance is the fact that those who practised it more regularly reported a greater increase in benefit overall. Subsequent to the delivery of this study, a further expanded eight-week course was developed and trialled in a number of state schools around the United Kingdom and in other European countries.

Incorporating Mindfulness Approaches

Bouncing Back & Coping with Change

Objectives

The 20 sessions can be delivered as a complete programme or selected as required for individuals, small groups or whole classes of children and young people. They have been designed to meet the following objectives:

- To increase self-esteem/self-concept.

- To increase participation in happy habits and the use of reframing and positive thinking.

- To enable students to understand how positive thinking and a positive attitude towards change can minimise stress and anxiety.

- To understand the nature and causes of stress in both general and personal terms.

- To understand how stress is person-specific.

- To increase co-operation and empathy with others and develop a growth mindset which is outward focused on others.

- To enable students to recognise their own optimum stress levels which allow for efficient functioning.

- To recognise reactions and behaviours which both reduce and increase stress and promote overall well-being.

- To understand and recognise the consequences of a range of stressors in both themselves and others.

- To develop joint problem-solving skills within a supportive framework and utilise effectively tools for relaxation and anxiety management (Cognitive Behavioural Therapy, mindfulness, Solution Focused (Brief) Therapy (SFBT), etc.).

- To encourage an understanding of how others view us and how this can/may impact upon both our self-esteem and our ability to cope with stress and tension in everyday life.

- To identify and develop a range of personal strategies to manage personal stressors and negative thinking patterns informed by relevant therapeutic approaches.

- To become more autonomous and feel more in control in all areas.

- To display the ability to savour the moment, show gratitude and engage in effective thinking.

- To understand the importance of emotional support from significant others (friends/ family etc.) in coping effectively with negative thinking.

- To understand how a healthy lifestyle can reduce stress/enable us to cope more effectively with a range of problems and still bounce back.

- To develop the ability to prioritise and organise both work and social agendas and to understand how this skill can reduce stress.

- To develop and practise assertiveness skills, understanding how such skills can aid in the management of stress.

- To understand how stress can adversely affect muscles and breathing and how making use of progressive relaxation can reduce such symptoms.

- To increase students' level of confidence in social interactions and in their own ability to cope with a range of more stressful situations and conflicts, while maintaining and developing positive relationships.

- To develop skills of reflection.

- To enable students to set realistic and considered personal goals.

- To improve students' ability to manage and cope effectively with stress and to consequently reduce current stress levels and anxieties.

Using the Sessions

Each of the 20 sessions follows a similar format and is designed to be delivered in approximately 45 to 60 minutes. Each session includes a series of activities and clear, straightforward instructions regarding delivery for the teacher or facilitator.

Apart from Session 1, all the sessions follow a similar format, as follows:

Introduction & Aims
To begin each session, reinforce the group rules as agreed in Session 1, and then outline the key aims for the session and briefly summarise the proposed activities.

Icebreaker – a Question to Thought-Storm
This question will reflect the main focus of the session and will encourage students to think more deeply about what they do and don't know, and to specifically highlight current levels of knowledge and understanding. This will also give the facilitator an idea as to how much input they may have to give when describing and introducing the key concepts and activities. The question is posed by the facilitator who will then encourage a group discussion whilst recording contributions (flip chart/white board/interactive white board) and summarising these as appropriate.

Warm-Up Game
It is important to explain the reason for engaging the students in such activities in these sessions. The idea is to present some unthreatening and co-operative warm-up games which will reinforce the need to empathise with others, build social skills and show the importance of forming and maintaining positive relationships. The importance of working co-operatively in a group may also be emphasised during this part of the session. Overall, it is hoped that these activities will reinforce the importance of simply having fun together and increasing our happiness quotient!

Activities

The activities (approximately 3 to 5 per session) are then worked through in turn. These incorporate a range of learning styles and ways of working – in pairs, whole group, individually, written, reflections, skills practice etc. There are clear instructions in each session plan regarding delivery and key concepts and ideas to be covered.

Feedback & Reflections

This part of the session enables the facilitator to ask the students to reflect upon what they have learnt in the session, posing the following questions:

- What was useful to you in this session?
- What might have made the session more useful to you?
- What have you learnt about yourself in today's session?
- What have you learnt about others?
- How will you use your knowledge and skills to help yourself and others in the future?

This is an important element of each session as it enables the students to really think about what they have learnt and the impact that this may have upon their overall well-being. Sharing their understanding of the key concepts covered and their own interpretations and learning can also serve to highlight differences and encourage the appreciation of diversity. This process can also highlight and reinforce the strategies and techniques that seem to work for the majority in terms of promoting and maintaining good emotional health.

A Mindful Moment

The final part of each session involves a mindfulness activity. Although Session 13 is entirely given over to this form of meditation, each session has a mindfulness activity, so it will be helpful to introduce this in some detail in Session 1. A script is provided in this first session, prior to introducing the activity, to ensure that students have some understanding of mindfulness as a way of maintaining and increasing well-being. It is, of course, vital that the facilitator also has a sound understanding of this approach and some experience of begin each session.

Mindfulness activities close each session in order to ensure that students leave in a peaceful, focused and secure way – it is hoped this will also be the case for those facilitating the sessions.

Success Criteria

It is hoped that the success of the programme can be measured in the following areas:

- Prompting school staff to reflect upon their practices and how these may impact upon student behaviour, self-esteem and social and emotional development - particularly in terms of developing personal coping strategies and problem-solving skills.
- Prompting a review of policies on self-esteem, emotional literacy and emotional support for pupils in order to further develop more inclusive whole-school approaches.

- Identifying any staff and pupil training needs in the areas of emotional awareness, mentoring, stress and anger management, assertiveness skills and basic counselling approaches.

- Enabling students to develop a more in-depth awareness of and understanding of their own feelings, attitudes and behaviours.

- Encouraging students to reflect more specifically upon their own feelings and behaviours, being able to recognise and articulate both negative and positive patterns.

- Increasing students' self-esteem/self-concept.

- Enabling students to understand and articulate the nature and causes of stress in both personal and more general terms and to acknowledge the fact that stress is person-specific.

- Helping students to understand how positive thinking can minimise stress and make appropriate use of this strategy.

- Increasing confidence, listening skills, assertive behaviours, co-operation and empathy.

- Increasing the ability of students to recognise their own and others optimal stress levels and the reactions and behaviours which both increase and reduce stress.

- Helping students to understand the importance of emotional support, a healthy lifestyle, and the development of organisational skills, relaxation techniques and assertiveness skills in coping effectively with stress; enabling students to make use of this range of strategies in the process.

- Enabling students to develop skills of reflection and consequently to develop and set realistic personal goals and targets.

- Removing the risk of students suffering from extreme levels of stress and withdrawing from the school context.

- Enabling students to develop the ability to transfer the skills and strategies taught into a range of social contexts.

- Enabling staff to increase their knowledge and awareness of the distinction between 'normal' and 'abnormal' levels of stress and to feel more confident in referring students on to appropriate specialist agencies at the appropriate time.

Session 1
The Happiness Habit

Introduction & Aims

In this session young people are introduced to the concepts of happiness and unhappiness as an experience common to all human beings in their daily lives. They're encouraged to reflect upon their own level of happiness and what triggers change in that level, as well as how they can further develop 'happy habits'. The notion that happiness is something we can work towards is also raised. The aims are:

- To define happiness and the ways in which we can increase our overall well-being and levels of happiness by developing, and consistently practising a range of 'happy habits'.

- To distinguish between real stress and the 'normal' stressors we would expect to encounter in our daily lives.

- To understand that life is full of ups and downs and challenges and happy times, but that we cannot expect to feel or be 'happy' all of the time.

- To reinforce the fact that happiness can be person specific.

- To formulate and clarify group rules for the sessions.

- For students to consider 10 keys to happier living and be able to visualise and articulate how they can make use of these in developing their own well-being.

It would be helpful to provide the young people with an outline of the programme. The main objectives can be reinforced in order to ensure that they fully understand the purpose of this series of skills-based sessions. These will be as follows:

- To provide students with a confidential and supportive framework in which they can begin to reflect upon their feelings, behaviours, actions and happiness levels.

- To allow each student in the group to begin to understand the nature and causes of stress both in themselves and others.

- To encourage students to distinguish between positive and negative responses to obstacles and challenges that we face.

- To encourage an understanding regarding the ways in which happiness and stress can be person specific.

- To increase students' awareness regarding the fact that people will need different levels of support at different times in their lives.

- To encourage students to further develop empathy for others alongside their own problem-solving skills within a supportive framework.

- To encourage students to consider and practise a range of strategies for coping with negative thinking and anxiety related to daily challenges and to consequently reduce their current stress levels and anxieties.

- To increase students' level of confidence and skill in social interactions and improve their own ability to cope with challenges and conflicts in an assertive and positive way.

- To increase students' knowledge of their own signature strengths and the ways in which they can build upon these.

- To develop a range of techniques and strategies to effectively manage and alter negative patterns of thinking, feeling and behaving which ultimately decrease our happiness levels and overall well-being.

- To boost positive emotions, gratitude, empathy, savouring skills, experiences of flow and a growth mindset which embraces challenge and change.

- To ensure that students are aware of the facilities and resources that are available to them should their life challenges become unmanageable in their daily lives, in other words how to self-refer or refer onto specialist therapeutic agencies as necessary.

It will also be useful for you to inform the students that each session will usually follow a similar format with an introduction, icebreaker, a warm-up game, activities, reflections and a mindfulness activity to close.

Icebreaker – A Question to Thought-Storm

Ask the question: 'What is happiness?'
Group members can then contribute their own ideas and definitions. These can be recorded on a whiteboard or flipchart as appropriate and it may then be useful for the group, as a whole, to formulate their own agreed definition. Students may wish to also focus upon some of the causes of happiness that they are currently experiencing in their lives.

Group Rules

The setting up of group rules is essential in terms of ensuring a positive tone and the safety and security of all young people involved in the programme. Ask the group to discuss and agree their own rules so as to ensure ownership of the sessions.

The rules may well include some of the following:

- We will all try to concentrate and be reflective in each session so that we can all contribute.

- We won't laugh at others or put them down.

- We'll listen to each other's ideas and show respect for them.

- We will take turns to talk.

- We will keep the privacy and confidentiality of the group.

- We will try to co-operate with each other at all times.
- We will choose not to say anything if we don't want to.

Disclosures

You may also wish to reinforce the fact that there may be things that are not appropriate to discuss within this group context. This would include any situation which would appear to be putting an individual young person at risk. Should such an issue arise, then it will be necessary to ensure that the student has access to one-to-one time with you or another appropriate adult in order to talk through the particular situation or difficulty. Disclosure of any abuse of any kind would obviously need to be dealt with via the usual support/ safeguarding system and referral mechanisms within the school.

Warm-Up Game

As this is the first warm-up game of the programme, it may be helpful for you to highlight the reason for engaging in these activities. The idea is to present some unthreatening and co-operative warm-up games which it is hoped will reinforce the need to empathise with others, build upon social skills and the importance of forming and maintaining positive relationships. The importance of working co-operatively in a group can also be emphasised during this part of the session. Overall, it is hoped that these activities will reinforce the importance of simply having fun together and increasing our happiness quotient!

The first warm-up game is 'A Chain Reaction'. This game requires the group to be alert and ready to respond to one another and is great fun when played at a really good pace. Ask everyone to stand in a circle. The idea is to end up with everyone sitting down. One person (A) is chosen to begin the game. They are asked to call out the name of another person (B) across the circle. Person A then sits down, Person B calls out the name of the third person (C) and Person B sits down. Person C calls out the name of a fourth person (D) and so on. If anyone hesitates or doesn't respond to being called, then the whole group has to stand up and the game begins again with a different person starting it off. This game is great fun, particularly when it is run at a rapid pace.

The aim is to see how fast the process can be completed and you could use a stopwatch or timer in order to establish a group record. The group can then attempt to break this record in future games.

Activities

1.1 My Happiness!

Ask the group to take a moment to think about what happiness means to them. Now ask them to record on the worksheet whatever comes into their heads so that they will be providing a truly authentic response. The worksheet contains two links for online resources which they may wish to follow up in order to measure their own levels of happiness at this point in time. These can form an initial assessment and provide a baseline level. The tests can then be repeated at the end of the programme to identify progress that has been made in further developing levels of overall well-being and happiness.

1.2 Getting the Happy Habit – Ten Top Tips for Happier Living

Worksheet 1.2 lists 10 Top Tips for happier living. The first five focus on how we interact with the outside world and the second five come from within us. Ask the group to look at these 10 top tips very carefully and then in smaller groups, to discuss what they understand each of these 'top tips' to mean for them in their lives.

1.3 My Happiness Shield

Give each group member a copy of Worksheet 1.3 showing the outline of a shield. Now ask them to write or draw on the shield all the things in their lives that make them happy or give them strength to cope with any difficulties that they may face. Explain that when things get difficult it can be helpful to visualise this shield and all that it means, so that they can remember to recall and use these strengths.

1.4 The Happiness Balance! 3:1

This activity introduces the work of Barbara Frederickson (2003) on the Happiness Ratio. She found that the ideal daily ratio of positive to negative emotions is 3:1 of positive to negative. This is the ratio that apparently ensures our overall well-being. So, it is important to ensure that for every negative emotion we experience on a daily basis, we also have three positive ones. Ask each member of the group to keep a daily diary for one week and try to record and count the positive and negative words/phrases they have used on each day. Once this is completed, they can try to calculate their 'happiness ratio' for each day and consider what this suggests about them and the way they live their lives.

1.5 Happy 5 Habits

This activity provides the students with a list of five things we can do to make ourselves happier. Give everyone a copy of the worksheet and then ask the group to look at each one, and then think about a personal target and strategy that they could use to achieve each target.

Feedback & Reflections

To close the session, ask the group to reflect upon what they have learnt during the session, posing the following questions:

- What was useful to you in this session?
- What might have made the session more useful to you?

- What have you learnt about yourself in today's session?

- What have you learnt about others?

- How will you use your knowledge and skills to help yourself and others in the future?

A Mindful Moment

When introducing this first mindfulness activity to the group, it is important for you to provide them with some additional background information. It may be helpful to initially define mindfulness as follows:

> Being mindful means paying attention to the present moment, exactly as it is. **It is really hard to be anxious if you are completely focused on the present moment** – what you are sensing and doing is ultimately right now. This is why it is so very important to learn how to use such tools and develop these skills – particularly in terms of helping ourselves to effectively deal with the normal stress and anxieties of everyday living.

You can then go on to describe mindfulness in the following terms:

> Being mindful is different from our usual behaviour when we are anxious: we tend to get stuck in our heads and think about everything that could go wrong. Our anxious brain likes to hang out in the unknown future and think about all the bad things that could happen. An anxious brain is very creative and can come up with the most amazing worst-case scenarios! Our anxious brain also likes to obsess about the past and dwell on regrets.

> When we dwell on the future and the past in this way, we are not able to notice the pleasant experiences all around us.

> For example, imagine you are learning how to sail. As you are getting into the boat, you decide that you are going to focus on the present instead of worrying about what will happen at school tomorrow. You feel the warm sun and cool breeze on your cheeks. You look up and watch the sail catch the wind above you. Maybe you smell the salt water and hear the seagulls as they circle above. As the speed of the boat increases, you enjoy the rush. All of your **senses are alive and focused on the present moment**. This is sailing in a mindful way.

> Mindfulness gives you a space **in the present moment** to be able to more safely deal with the distressing and painful memories of things that might have happened to you in the past. It also allows you to look at and plan for the future, even when you might have fearful thoughts about things that haven't yet happened, from a secure position of knowing that you are in the present moment. In fact, we are never NOT in the present moment – we just lose track of that fact quite often. Sometimes it is easier to understand something in terms of what it is **not**.

Here are some examples of mindLESSness:

- Breaking things, spilling things, clumsiness, accidents because of carelessness, inattention or thinking about something else.

- Failing to notice subtle or not-so-subtle feelings such as physical discomfort, pain, tension.

- Forgetting someone's name as soon as you hear it.

- Listening to someone with one ear while doing something else at the same time.

- Getting so focused on goals that you lose touch with what you are doing right now.

- Getting lost in your thoughts and feelings.

- Being preoccupied with the future or the past.

- Eating without being aware of eating.

- Having periods of time where you have difficulty remembering the details of what happened – running on autopilot.

- Reacting emotionally in certain ways – feeling like an emotion 'just came out of nowhere'.

- Daydreaming or thinking of other things when doing chores.

- Doing several things at once rather than focusing on one thing at a time.

- Distracting yourself with things like eating, alcohol, pornography, drugs, and work.

If you do most or even some of these things at times, then you are probably a normal member of the human race.

The first mindfulness activity therefore, is simply a means of enabling the group to see how they can focus on the here and now. The 'Three Senses Activity' helps them to simply notice what they are experiencing right now through three senses – sound, sight, touch.

First, ask the students to take a few slow breaths and ask themselves:

- What are three things I can hear? (clock on the wall, car going by, music in the next room, my breath)

- What are three things I can see? (this table, that sign, that person walking by)

- What are three things I can feel? (the chair under me, the floor under my feet, my phone in my pocket)

Now ask them to slowly think of their own personal answers, one sense at a time.

It's impossible to do this exercise and not be present and mindful!

1.1 My Happiness!

Take a moment to think about what happiness *means* to you. Write or draw whatever comes into your head.

What does happiness mean to you?

Example: Feeling good about how things are going

Now think about specific things that often make you happy. These could be activities, people, places or anything else that comes to mind.

What things make you happy?

Example: A relaxing day out with my best friend

These links are to questionnaires that can help you to assess your levels of happiness. Why not try them now, and then once again when you have completed these sessions, and see if there is a difference in the results.

a) Your overall level of happiness with life (General Happiness Scale):
    www.authentichappiness.sas.upenn.edu/ testcenter

b) Your current mood (PANAS – Positive & Negative Affect – Questionnaire):
    www.authentichappiness.sas.upenn.edu/ testcenter

1.2 Getting the Happy Habit

Ten Top Tips to Happier Living

The first 5 tips focus on how we interact with the OUTSIDE world and the second 5 tips come from WITHIN us!

Look at these 10 top tips very carefully…

GIVING	Do things for others
RELATING	Connect with people
EXERCISING	Take care of your body
APPRECIATING	Notice the world around
TRYING OUT	Keep learning new things
DIRECTION	Have goals to look forward to
RESILIENCE	Find ways to bounce back
EMOTION	Take a positive approach
ACCEPTANCE	Be comfortable with who you are
MEANING	Be part of something bigger

In smaller groups discuss what you understand each of these Top Tips to mean for you in your life.

1.3 My Happiness Shield

1.4 The Happiness Balance!

3:1

Barbara Frederickson (2003) has researched the happiness ratio. The ideal ratio of positive to negative emotions on a daily basis is 3:1, positive to negative. This ratio ensures well-being. So, it is important to ensure that for every negative emotion you experience, you have three positive ones!!

Daily Diary

Keep a daily diary for one week and record and count the positive and negative words/ phrases you have used on each day. Try to calculate your 'happiness ratio' for each day and consider what this suggests about you and the way you live your life.

Day	Positive words/ phrases	Negative words/ phrases	Happiness ratio	What does this say about me?
Sunday				
Monday				
Tuesday				
Wednesday				
Thursday				
Friday				
Saturday				

1.5 Happy 5 Habits

In the table below are 5 things we can do to make ourselves happier. Look at each one and then think about a personal target and strategy that you could use to achieve each target.

	My target	My strategy
1. Make lots of friends and be kind to them.		
2. Be grateful for what you have every day.		
3. Don't compare yourself badly with others.		
4. Don't compare yourself to those in the media or famous personalities.		
5. Savour your experiences.		

Thinking of Others

Introduction & Aims

To start, reinforce the group rules as agreed in Session 1, and then outline the key aims for the session and briefly summarise the proposed activities.

The aims of this session are:

- To define and understand the concept of empathy.
- To reflect upon feelings associated with key events and people in your lives.
- To identify the ways that we can show our feelings for others and demonstrate to them that we care about them.
- To understand how and why doing acts for kindness for others is good for us.
- To devise and deliver random acts of kindness and understand how doing good for others can reinforce our own sense of well-being.

Icebreaker - A Question to Thought-Storm

Ask the question: 'What is empathy and why is it important for us to develop this characteristic?'

Ask everyone to contribute their own ideas and definitions. These can be written on a whiteboard or flipchart and it may then be useful for the group, as a whole, to come up with their own agreed definition. Group members may also wish to focus upon some of the empathy that they have shown to others and the times when others have been empathetic towards them.

Warm-Up Game

Imagine the Line

In this game, ask everyone to from a circle and then imagine that there is a line through the middle of the circle, forming a scale, as if from 0 to 10. Now explain that you are going to read out two opposing statements. The group members should stand on the line at one end or the other, or in the middle, according to where they think they are on the scale. It may be helpful to actually number the scale from 0 to 10 using chalk or, alternatively, place large sheets of paper which are numbered along the line in the centre of the circle. You can then read out a series of statements, remembering to indicate which end of this imaginary line is which. For example:

- I love eating any food … I'm very picky about what I eat.

- I always feel angry and argue with people … I never feel angry and argue with people.

- I love playing football … I hate playing football.

- I enjoy art lessons … I totally dislike art lessons.

- I'm very neat in my work … I'm very messy in my work.

- I get on well with my friends … I don't get on well with my friends.

Be sure to reinforce the fact that there are no right or wrong answers here. The idea is to highlight the fact that we are all similar and we are all different.

Activities

2.1 My Main Experiences

In this activity, the group are asked to list the main places, people and activities in their lives and to then record the feelings that go with each of these on the chart provided. This activity is designed to reinforce the fact that we all have people and situations/contexts in our lives which can evoke both comfortable and uncomfortable feelings and emotions.

2.2 Thought-Storm: Showing that We are Thinking of Others

Ask the group to engage in a thought-storm activity which poses the following questions:
How do we think of others?
How do we show that we think about them and/or care for them?

The students can work independently at first, and then with others in the group. They can then reflect upon the final two questions:
Do we share similar definitions and ideas?
Do we show how we feel and care for others in similar ways?

2.3.1 Acts of Kindness

Introduce the idea that doing things to help others is good for us and for those who we help. As the saying goes: 'If you want to feel good, do good'. They are therefore encouraged to perform an act of kindness each day. This could be paying someone a compliment, giving a helping hand, a hug, a gift or something else. The act might be large or small and the recipient may not even be aware of it. Ideally these acts of kindness should be beyond the kind things you already do on a regular basis. On the worksheet are some ideas for acts of kindness as a prompt to their own thinking. Ask everyone to read them through and then tick any that they have already done. Now think of some other acts of kindness they might have done that are not on the list.

2.3.2 Random Acts of Kindness Diary

The diary format enables the group to next record at least one kind act each day for a week and to try to do a different one each day. They can use this format to keep a record of their acts of kindness and can also note down how they felt when doing them and whether they found them easy or difficult.

Feedback & Reflections

Ask the group to reflect upon what they have learnt in the session, posing the following questions:

- What was useful for you in this session?
- What might have made the session more useful for you?
- What have you learnt about yourself in today's session?
- What have you learnt about others?
- How will you use your knowledge and skills to help yourself and others in the future?

A Mindful Moment

Observe your thoughts on the train line - let them move on and reduce that stress!

Ask the group to sit mindfully and then read the following script to them:

Sit quietly and close your eyes and visualise yourself in the countryside on the side of a hill. Look down and see the train track and visualise a train moving along that track. Look carefully at each carriage as it goes past and think of it as one of your thoughts. If you get caught up in your thought and feel as if you've jumped onto the carriage, gently get back up to the top of the hill. Let that thought 'go' – notice it but don't get on the carriage. Move on in your mind and reduce that stress!

Session 2 Thinking of Others

2.1 My Main Experiences

List the main places, people and activities in your life. Then record the feelings that go with each of these on the chart below.

Place, Person, Activity	Feelings

Which give you the most comfortable feelings?

Which give you the most uncomfortable feelings?

2.2 Thought-Storm: Showing that We Are Thinking Of Others

How do we think of others?
How do we show that we think about them and care for them?

Work on your own at first, and then with others in the group.

Do we share similar definitions and ideas?

Do we show how we feel and care for others in similar ways?

2.3 Acts of Kindness

Doing things to help others is good for us and for those who we help!
As the saying goes: 'If you want to feel good, do good'!

Perform an act of kindness each day for a week.

This could be paying a compliment, giving a helping hand, a hug, a gift or something else.
The act may be large or small and the recipient may not even be aware of it.

Ideally your acts of kindness should be beyond the kind things you already do on a regular basis. And of course the acts mustn't put you or others in danger!

Do at least one extra kind act each day for a week, ideally a different one each day.
Here are some ideas for acts of kindness:

- [ ] Giving up your place in the lunch queue for someone who is in a rush.
- [ ] Holding a door open for someone.
- [ ] Giving a (sincere) compliment.
- [ ] Making someone laugh.
- [ ] Giving someone a hug.
- [ ] Taking the time to really listen to someone.
- [ ] Making someone new feel welcome.
- [ ] Let one person in front of you in every queue.
- [ ] Give directions to someone who is lost.
- [ ] Have a chat with someone in your class who looks left out or a bit sad.
- [ ] Pick up litter as you walk.
- [ ] Let someone in front of you in the supermarket queue.
- [ ] Tell someone they mean a lot to you.
- [ ] Let someone have your seat on the bus.
- [ ] Read a story with a child.
- [ ] Offer your change to someone struggling to find the right amount.
- [ ] Treat a loved one to breakfast in bed.
- [ ] Buy cakes or sweets for your friends.
- [ ] Invite your neighbour round for tea and a chat.
- [ ] Offer to help with someone's shopping.

- [ ] Tell someone if you notice they're doing something well.
- [ ] Pass on a book you've enjoyed.
- [ ] Say sorry (you know who to).
- [ ] Forgive someone for what they've done.
- [ ] Visit a sick friend, relative or neighbour.
- [ ] Buy an unexpected gift for someone.
- [ ] Make something for a neighbour.
- [ ] Pay for someone in the queue behind you.
- [ ] Do a chore or job around the house that you don't normally do.
- [ ] Help out someone in need.
- [ ] Offer to look after a friend's pet.
- [ ] Offer to mow an older neighbour's lawn.
- [ ] Donate your old things to charity.
- [ ] Give food to a homeless person and take time to talk with them.
- [ ] Visit someone who may be lonely.
- [ ] Take your old clothes to a charity shop.
- [ ] Get back in contact with someone you've lost touch with.
- [ ] Organise a fundraising event.
- [ ] Volunteer your time for a charity.
- [ ] Plan a surprise party for a friend.

Make a tick against any of these Acts that you have already completed once in your life and then think of some that are not on this list that you have done!

2.3.2 Random Acts of Kindness Diary

Try to do at least one kind act each day for a week and to do a different one each day.

Use this diary to keep a record of your acts of kindness. You can also note down how you felt about doing them and whether you found them easy or difficult.

I. Date:
What did you do? Who for? How did it go?

2. Date:
What did you do? Who for? How did it go?

3. Date:
What did you do? Who for? How did it go?

4. Date:
What did you do? Who for? How did it go?

5. Date:
What did you do? Who for? How did it go?

6. Date:
What did you do? Who for? How did it go?

7. Date:
What did you do? Who for? How did it go?

Session 3
Being in the Flow

Introduction & Aims

To start, reinforce the group rules as agreed in Session 1, and then outline the key aims for the session and briefly summarise the proposed activities.

The aims of this session are:

- To understand the concept of flow and how we can experience this in our lives.
- To understand the benefits of the flow experiences we have.
- To recognise how we can use our strengths and skills to reframe boring activities.
- To proactively plan to engage in flow activities and reflect upon these on a weekly basis.

Icebreaker - A Question to Thought-Storm

Ask the question: 'What is flow and when do we experience this?'
It will be helpful provide a definition of 'flow' in this context, highlighting that we experience 'flow' when we are engaged in activities to such an extent that we do not feel time pass or have any idea of what is going on around us. It is simply a state of total absorption and can be hugely fulfilling.

Ask everyone to contribute their own ideas and definitions. These can be written on a whiteboard or flipchart and it may then be useful for the group, as a whole, to come up with their own agreed definition. Ask group members to focus upon some of the flow experiences they have had and highlight any similarities or differences in these experiences.

Warm-Up Game

Pass the Ball
The game promotes careful looking skills and co-operation. Ask everyone to stand close together, in a circle facing inwards. One person is then chosen to stand in the middle of the circle. Everyone else passes the ball around the circle behind their backs. The person in the centre must guess where the ball is. When they think they know where the ball is they can shout 'Stop!'. Everyone in the circle must then stand still while the centre person makes two guesses as to where they think the ball may be. If they are correct, they can swap places with the person who has the ball. If they guess wrongly, then the game resumes and they can have up to three turns at guessing.

In order to make this slightly more difficult, two objects can be passed around the circle simultaneously. The person in the centre will then have to guess where both objects are after they have shouted 'Stop!'.

Activities

3.1 Flow

For this activity, explain how Csikszentmihalyi identified the concept of Flow in the 1960s while doing research into the creative process (Seligman & Csikszentmihalyi, 2000). He noticed how artists would ignore hunger, discomfort and tiredness when they were working on their paintings. They were 'in the flow' and totally involved in the activity to the exclusion of everything and everyone else. Ask the group to identify their own 'flow' activities and to record these on their worksheets. In pairs or small groups, spend some time comparing ideas and try to identify any similarities and differences in their responses.

3.2 Turning Boring Activities into Interesting & Challenging Ones

For this activity, the group must come up with ideas for trying to turn what they perceive to be boring activities into more challenging ones. How might they do this? Ask everyone to try to think of some creative responses and to focus on the fact that we can use our own strengths and creativity to challenge ourselves and reframe tasks that can seem boring and dull. Write the activities and new ideas on the worksheet and share the most creative responses with the group.

3.2 My Flow Daily Diary

Give everyone a copy of the 'My Flow Daily Diary' worksheet and explain that they are to use this diary to plan as many flow times as possible over the next week – times when they have lots of pleasure and lots of mastery and experience being in the flow! This will hopefully encourage them to plan to do those activities that revitalise and energise them!

Feedback & Reflections

Ask the group to reflect upon what they have learnt in the session, posing the following questions:

- What was useful for you in this session?
- What might have made the session more useful for you?
- What have you learnt about yourself in today's session?
- What have you learnt about others?
- How will you use your knowledge and skills to help yourself and others in the future?

A Mindful Moment

Relax by the River

Ask the group to sit mindfully and read the following script to them:

Close your eyes and be very still and peaceful. Then imagine you are lying in a boat and floating slowly and peacefully down the river. Lie back in the boat on a pile of soft cushions and allow the gentle breeze to blow over your face and the river to move you along in a tranquil way. Let your whole body become very still and feel the sunshine on your face and body. Rest and be at peace. Listen to the birds sing and feel the water gently lapping against the side of the boat. Feel at peace and, as you lie there, let all the muscles in your body relax.

Breathe in and out and feel yourself sinking deeper and deeper into a peaceful and happy place.

3.1 Flow

Csikszentmihalyi identified the concept of Flow in the 1960s when he was doing research into the creative process. He noticed how artists would ignore hunger, discomfort and tiredness when they were working on their paintings. They were said to be 'in the flow' and totally involved in their activity to the exclusion of everything and everyone else.

What are your 'flow' activities?

Write or draw them in the box below.

3.2 Turning Boring Activities into Interesting & Challenging Ones

Activities I Find Boring	Ways I can make them interesting and challenging!
1.	
2.	
3.	
4.	
5.	

3.3 My Flow Daily Diary

Use this diary to plan as many flow times as possible over the next week – times when you have lots of pleasure and lots of mastery and experience being in the flow! Plan to do those activities that revitalise and energise you!

	Monday	Tuesday	Wednesday	Thursday	Friday	Saturday	Sunday
9.00am							
11.00am							
1.00pm							
3.00pm							
5.00pm							
7.00pm							
9.00pm							
11.00pm							

Session 4
Developing Grit – The 'Tigger' Effect

Introduction & Aims

To start, reinforce the group rules as agreed in Session 1, and then outline the key aims for this session and briefly summarise the proposed activities.

The aims of this session are:

- To understand the concept of grit and the need to develop this character trait.

- To identify the group's current levels of grit and the skills that they need to develop still further in order to be able to stick at things when the going gets difficult.

- To recognise how and when others have demonstrated grit and the importance of not being stereotyped or limited by the labels we give ourselves or the preconceptions of others.

- To make use of a visual tool to develop a vision of a desired outcome and identify and problem-solve around any obstacles to this.

Icebreaker - A Question to Thought-Storm

Ask the group the question: 'What is 'grit'?'
Ask everyone to contribute their own ideas and definitions. These can be written on a whiteboard or flipchart and it may then be useful for the group, as a whole, to come up with their own agreed definition.

Ask the group to think about some of the times when they have been stuck at something that they found quite difficult but kept going until the job was complete. They should try to think about and identify what skills and strengths they were drawing upon in order to be able to persist – even in the face of very real difficulties.

Warm-Up Game

The Chair Game

Arrange chairs in a circle, one for each person. Then take away one of the chairs and ask for a volunteer to stand in the middle. Everyone else sits on their chair. The person in the middle should attempt to sit down whilst the others change places as you call out commands, such as:

Swap places if you:
- Have changed your hair this year.
- Had cereal for breakfast.
- Came to school by bus.
- Are wearing black socks.
- Feel happy today.

Group members can contribute their own ideas for reasons to swap places.

When the person in the middle manages to get a chair, the person left standing can take their place.

Activities

4.1 Developing Grit

In this activity the group are encouraged to consider their own levels of 'grit' and to measure themselves against a series of key statements which will reveal their levels of 'stickability' and determination not to give up – even when the going gets tough. Give everyone a copy of the worksheet and ask them to read the statements and then rate each using the following ratings: Totally True (TT), Mainly True of Me (MT) and Not True of Me (NT).

4.2 Develop Grit to Succeed

In this activity, the focus is on developing the group members' awareness of their own skills and strengths still further. First, ask them to think about the following key questions: How can you persevere when things get tough? What strengths can you use? Then ask them to draw themselves in the picture frame and record all their strengths around the outside.

4.3 Mission Impossible – They Did It! People Who Used True Grit to Overcome Obstacles and Problems!

Ask students to form small groups and work together to look at the statements on the worksheet and find the evidence to show that they are false. For example, Richard Branson came bottom of his class, was dyslexic and left school at 16 but he is now a world renowned multi-millionaire businessman. They need to work together in order to find someone who shows each statement to be false.

4.4 The Story of My Hero

Explain that you want the group to write the story of someone who they think of as a hero. This can be someone they know, or someone they have heard of in the media. They can use the following questions to help them with ideas and prompt their thinking:

- What has the person done to make you respect them so much and what are the obstacles that they needed to overcome?

- What was the effort that went into their accomplishments?

- How did they show 'true grit' and stick with the plan even when the going got tough?

4.5 Using the Cartoon Storyboard Technique – Use Grit to Solve That Problem!

This technique of storyboarding was developed by Jane Henry (Mayle, 2006) and is a visual tool to help develop a vision of a desired outcome and to identify and problem solve around any obstacles to this. Encourage the group to think of a goal they would like to achieve and then to make use of the six boxes provided on the worksheet in order to solve any problems and overcome any obstacles to reaching their goal.

Feedback & Reflections

Ask the group to reflect upon what they have learnt in the session, posing the following questions:

- What was useful for you in this session?

- What might have made the session more useful for you?

- What have you learnt about yourself in today's session?

- What have you learnt about others?

- How will you use your knowledge and skills to help yourself and others in the future?

A Mindful Moment - Mindful Breathing!

Ask the group to find a comfortable place to sit, closing their eyes and making their spines as straight as possible. Now read the following script:

Now you are comfortable and still, focus your attention on your breathing. When a thought or emotion pops into your head accept it, but then allow it to float on by (imagine you are pinning them to a cloud or onto a leaf floating down the river). Focus your attention on the rise and fall of your chest, the feeling of the air entering and leaving your body.
This is mindful breathing. Keep practising and use it every day!

4.1 Developing Grit

Read the statements and then rank them as either:
Totally True (TT) Mainly True of Me (MT) Not True of Me (NT)

Interests	
My interests change from year to year or month to month.	
I have been very interested in an idea or a hobby for a short time but then I lost interest.	
I have difficulty keeping my focus on an activity that takes a long time to finish.	
I often set a goal but I sometimes change my mind and choose another one.	
New ideas and new activities take my mind off previous ones.	
I become interested in new hobbies or activities every few months.	

Effort	
I have achieved a goal that took me a long time and lots of hard work.	
I have overcome setbacks and difficulties to meet a challenge.	
I finish whatever task or activity I begin.	
Setbacks don't put me off.	
I am a hard worker.	
I am a careful worker.	

(Adapted from Duckworth et al., 2007)

4.2 Develop Grit to Succeed

Think about these questions:
How can you persevere when things get tough?
What strengths can you use?

Draw yourself in the picture frame and write or draw all of your strengths around the outside.

4.3 Mission Impossible - They Did It! People Who Used True Grit to Overcome Obstacles and Problems!

Working together in a small group, look at the statements on the cards and try to come up with evidence to show that they are FALSE!

For example, Richard Branson came bottom of his class, was dyslexic and left school at 16 but he is now a world renowned multi-millionaire businessman.

For each statement, try to find someone who shows it to be false!

You won't get a good job if you come bottom of the class.	Dreamers don't get anywhere	People without arms or legs cannot win Olympic medals
You can't run a business from your bedroom	You can't be a great novelist if your book has been turned down by 20 publishers	Women with children can't be successful in business
You can't be a famous singer if you have special needs	You can only become a celebrity by going on TV reality shows	You can't become a boxer if you are already a great cricketer
	A woman cannot be a Prime Minister	A black person cannot be President of the USA

4.4 The Story of My Hero

Write the story of someone whom you think of as a hero. Use these questions to help your ideas.

What has the person done to make you respect them so much and what are the obstacles that they needed to overcome?

What was the effort that went into their accomplishments?

How did they show 'true grit' and stick with the plan even when the going got tough?

THE STORY OF MY HERO

4.5 Using the Cartoon Storyboard Technique - Use Grit to Solve That Problem!

Think of a goal that you would like to achieve and then use the six boxes below to help you to solve any problems and overcome any obstacles to reaching that goal.

1. My goal and the problems/obstacles to reaching it.	2. Step 1 I can take to reaching a solution.
3. Step 2 I can take to reaching a solution.	4. Step 3 I can take to reaching a solution.
5. Step 4 I can take to reaching a solution.	6. How I would feel if I overcame the problems and reached my goal?

Session 5
Building My Strengths

Introduction & Aims

To start, reinforce the group rules as agreed in Session 1, and then outline the key aims for the session and briefly summarise the proposed activities.

The aims of this session are:

- To understand the concept of personal strengths and the notion of 'character strength' as being something we can all use in times of stress and to further build our ability to bounce back.
- To be able to assess personal strengths.
- To identify how to further build upon strengths.
- To understand how we use these strengths in our daily lives.

Icebreaker – A Question to Thought-Storm

Ask the question: 'What is a personal strength?'
Ask everyone to contribute their own ideas and definitions. These can be written on a whiteboard or flipchart and it may then be useful for the group, as a whole, to come up with their own agreed definition.

The group may wish to also focus upon some of strengths they have which they know have helped them to overcome difficulties or meet challenges in their lives.

Warm-Up Game

The Shape Game
This is a game in which the group are encouraged to work together and focus on further developing co-operation skills. For this activity you will need stickers of different shapes, e.g., circles, stars, triangles, moons or different coloured stickers of the same shape. Without letting the students see the shape or colour you are using, place one sticker on each person's forehead. Now everyone must find others with the same shape or colour sticker as their own and form into groups. For example, all the circles together, all the stars together. However, they are not allowed to talk or mime what someone's shape is. Time how quickly they are able to get into the correct groups. Follow the activity with a discussion

Session 5 Building My Strengths

focusing on how it felt to be helped and supported by others, and reinforcing the fact that all of us need help and support at various times and for various reasons.

Activities

5.1 Martin Seligman's 24 Character Strengths

Give each group member a copy of Worksheet 5.1 which lists the 24 character strengths as identified the psychologist, Martin Seligman (Peterson & Seligman, 2004). Using their own words, everyone must come up with a definition for each strength. They can work on their own, or with partners and can make use of a dictionary or online resource. When everyone has finished, definitions can be fed back to the group and compared to see if people have come up with similar definitions.

5.2 Sort the Strengths! A Self-reflection Exercise

This is a self-reflection activity in which the group are again given a worksheet listing character strengths. Ask everyone to cut out the strengths and then rank them in order showing which are their greatest strengths and their weakest. It may be helpful to discuss their rankings with a partner. Do they agree with each other's personal assessments?

5.3 Seligman's 24 Character Strengths - Working on My 5 Lowest Strengths

In this final activity of the session, ask the group to reflect upon their five lowest strengths and to consider how they might be able to further build upon these.
Can they use their greatest strengths to support them in the process?
Can other people support them and how?

Feedback & Reflections

Ask the group to reflect upon what they have learnt in the session, posing the following questions:

- What was useful for you in this session?
- What might have made the session more useful for you?
- What have you learnt about yourself in today's session?
- What have you learnt about others?
- How will you use your knowledge and skills to help yourself and others in the future?

A Mindful Moment

Being still!

Read the following script to the group once they are sitting mindfully:

Focus and be still. Feel all your attention gently falling from the top of your head down to your neck, lightly falling like a petal or a leaf falling from a tree. Feel your attention move down through your shoulders … your arms … your hands … your chest and belly … your hips and thighs … your knees and ankles … into your feet and all the way down to your toes.

Let your mind rest in your body, noticing all the feelings inside – tingling, shivers, warmth, coolness, relaxation, tightness or nothing at all. Notice how the sensations and feelings change when you bring attention to them. See if you can feel the stillness in your body as you sit, not moving, and noticing changing sensations throughout your body.

Adapted from Goodman (2005, p. 217)

Session 5 Building My Strengths

5.1 Martin Seligman's 24 Character Strengths

The list below shows the 24 different character strengths as identified by Martin Seligman, a famous psychologist.

Use a dictionary, online resource, or work with a partner to come up with a definition for each strength using your own words.

Now compare your definitions with the rest of the group – how similar are they?

1. Creativity   _____

2. Curiosity   _____

3. Open-mindedness   _____

4. Love of learning   _____

5. Keeping perspective _____

6. Bravery   _____

7. Persistence   _____

8. Integrity   _____

9. Vitality   _____

10. Love   _____

11. Kindness   _____

12. Social intelligence _____

13. Citizenship   _____

14. Fairness   _____

15. Leadership   _____

16. Forgiveness   _____

17. Humility   _____

18. Prudence   _____

19. Self-regulation   _____

20. Appreciation of beauty _____

21. Gratitude   _____

22. Hope   _____

23. Humour   _____

24. Spirituality   _____

5.2 Sort the Strengths!
A Self-Reflection Exercise

Cut out the strengths listed below and then rank these in order, thinking about which are your greatest strengths and which are your 'weakest' strengths.

Discuss your ranking with a partner, do they agree with your choices?

Creativity	Citizenship	Integrity	Appreciation of beauty
Curiosity	Fairness	Vitality	Gratitude
Open-mindedness	Leadership	Love	Hope
Love of learning	Forgiveness	Kindness	Humour
Keeping perspective	Humility	Social intelligence	Spirituality
Bravery	Prudence	Persistence	Self-regulation

5.3 Seligman's 24 Character Strengths: Working on My 5 Lowest Strengths

Think about the five character strengths you identified as your weakest.
How might you improve these strengths? Who could help you to do this?

My five weakest strengths	Things I can do to improve these
1.	
2.	
3.	
4.	
5.	

Session 6
My Feelings

Introduction & Aims

To start, reinforce the group rules as agreed in Session 1, and then outline the key aims for the session and briefly summarise the proposed activities.

The aims of this session are:

- To define feelings and distinguish between uncomfortable and comfortable feelings.
- To consider how uncomfortable feelings such as shame and guilt can be positive in terms of prompting us to change our behaviour, act differently or make amends for something that we have done wrong.
- To further reinforce the importance of developing empathy.
- To begin to understand how our thoughts, feelings and behaviours are connected.

Icebreaker - A Question to Thought-storm

Ask the question: 'What are feelings?'
Ask everyone to contribute their own ideas and definitions. These can be written on a whiteboard or flipchart and it may then be useful for the group, as a whole, to come up with their own agreed definition.

Group members may wish to also focus upon some of the causes of both the uncomfortable and comfortable feelings that they are currently experiencing in their lives. It may also be helpful to consider why uncomfortable feelings such as shame and guilt can be positive in terms of prompting us to change our behaviour, act differently or make amends for something that we have done wrong.

Warm-up Game

The Rainbow
Ask the group to sit in the circle and then name each person around the circle using the colours of the rainbow – red, orange, yellow, green, blue, indigo and violet. Now call out one or two different colours. Anyone with these colours must change places. If you call out 'Rainbow!' the whole group must change places.

Activities

6.1 Feeling Cards

Give each person a copy of worksheet 6.1 and ask them to cut out the cards, which contain a range of scenarios involving different people, e.g., 'The prime minister being booed at a conference', 'An old lady being mugged'. Working in pairs or in the whole group, ask them to select a card and for each scenario ask them to consider the following:

How does the person feel? How would you feel in the same situation?

The idea is to highlight the importance of developing empathy – being able to put ourselves in someone else's shoes.

6.2 Circle Time Reflections: How Would You Feel If…?

Give everyone a copy of worksheet 6.2 and ask the group to talk in a circle time or class discussion about each statement on the worksheet, and then say how they would feel, and why, if the statement applied to them.

Now ask each person to think of three more situations and to identify how they might cope best in each of these.

6.3 Empathy Matters

This activity reinforces the importance of developing empathy and asks the group to consider the following question in relation to a number of scenarios: How would I feel if I was in your shoes?

You can prepare the scenarios in advance by making a selection of pictures from newspapers and magazines which show young and old people in a variety of difficult situations. Using a circle time session to reflect upon each picture is probably the best option to facilitate the discussion and address each question in turn.

6.4 Reflect! My Thoughts & Feelings Diary – Thinking About How our Thoughts and Feelings are Connected

In this thoughts and feelings diary, the group are asked to keep a daily record of significant situations which prompted strong feelings for them. The idea is to begin to analyse the triggers for these feelings with a view to being able to develop strategies to manage or replace them with more appropriate or healthy ones. Ask everyone to record under the following headings on the diary worksheet:

- Day and Time

- The Situation: Where, when and who with?

- Thoughts : Which were 'hot', in other words, the strongest?

- Feelings: How were you feeling?

Feedback 4 Reflections

Ask the group to reflect upon what they have learnt in the session, posing the following questions:

- What was useful for you in this session?
- What might have made the session more useful for you?
- What have you learnt about yourself in today's session?
- What have you learnt about others?
- How will you use your knowledge and skills to help yourself and others in the future?

A Mindful Moment – The First Time!

Read the following script to the group as they lie down in a space on the floor.

Close your eyes and pay attention to your breathing, following the breath as it goes in and out. [Pause for a minute.]

After a while, pay attention to your body, one part at a time, noticing any sensations of cold, hot, tight or anything else that you can identify. After some time of attention to your body, start listening to the sounds of the room, without judging, criticising or even thinking about them. Simply listen. Then slowly open your eyes and look around. Look carefully and with interest as if you are seeing the room for the first time. Stop and then rest your eyes on an object for half a minute. Examine it without saying things about it in your mind.

At the conclusion, bring the group's attention back by ringing a bell.

6.1 Feeling Cards

Cut out the cards and read through the different scenarios on the cards. For each card think carefully about the following questions:

How does the person feel in this situation?

How would you feel in the same situation?

✂

Beyonce singing to an adoring audience.	The prime minister being booed at a conference.	An old lady being mugged.
A traveller girl being beaten up.	A young woman walking home alone late at night.	An old man peering through the curtain at a gang outside.
A miner in a tunnel.	A disabled teenager watching a football match.	A new student in your class/form.
A young teacher having difficulties controlling the class.	A shopkeeper being racially abused.	A child at a funeral.
A girl pushing off a boy.	A boy watching two others smoking a joint.	A refugee watching other kids playing football.
Two drunk girls falling over a pram in the street.	A suicide bomber walking through a crowd.	A fat boy being bullied.
A Muslim girl having her veil pulled off by a boy.	Two gay men holding hands.	A man who has been beaten up after a night at the pub.
A girl in a new BMW.	Someone getting married.	A young boy whose parents/carers are fighting.

✂ Ⓟ This page may be photocopied for instructional use only. *Bouncing Back & Coping With Change* © Tina Rae 2016

6.2 Circle Time Reflections

How Would You Feel if...?

Talk in a circle time or class discussion about each statement and then say how you would feel (and why) if…

- You were the only black child in your class.
- You were unable to hear.
- You couldn't walk and you were paralysed from the waist down.
- You didn't have nice clothes.
- You were really poor.
- You were really rich.
- Your sister had cerebral palsy.
- No one spoke your language at school.
- You couldn't read or write as well as the other kids in your class.
- You didn't have any friends.
- You were the only person in your class who believed in God and practised your religion.

Can you think of three more?

1 _____

2 _____

3 _____

Think how you might cope best in three of these situations!

1 _____

2 _____

3 _____

6.3 Empathy Matters

'How would I feel if I was in your shoes?'

Look at the selection of pictures from newspapers and magazines showing young and old people in a variety of difficult situations.

Reflect upon each picture and think about:

How is this person feeling?

How can we tell?

What is happening?

What would we feel like in their shoes?

Can this situation be 'put right'?

What might help?

6.4 Reflect! My Thoughts & Feelings Diary
Thinking About How Our Thoughts and Feelings are Connected

Day and Time	The Situation: Where, when and who with?	Thoughts: Which were 'hot' i.e., the strongest?	Feelings How were you feeling?

Session 7

Beat the Stress

Introduction & Aims

To start, reinforce the group rules as agreed in Session 1, and then outline the key aims for the session and briefly summarise the proposed activities.

The aims of this session are:

- To define stress and the person-specific nature of stress.
- To develop a healthy attitude to managing stress and identify the healthiest options for doing this.
- To understand the need to organise workloads effectively.
- To learn about strategies for managing stressors.
- To identify the main stressors group members encounter on a weekly basis and identify triggers and potential coping mechanisms.

Icebreaker - A Question to Thought-storm

Ask the question: 'What is stress?'
Ask everyone to contribute their own ideas and definitions. These can be written on a whiteboard or flipchart and it may then be useful for the group, as a whole, to come up with their own agreed definition.

Group members may also wish to focus upon some of the causes of stress that they are currently experiencing in their lives and reflect upon any differences or similarities in these experiences. This may help to highlight the fact that stress is person specific and that individuals cope differently with such experiences. It may also be helpful to focus on the ways in which a certain amount of stress can be helpful to us in terms of prompting us to identify and complete tasks and projects.

Warm-up Game

The Balloon Game
This game aims to allow each person to feel part of the group, while also encouraging a sense of power for the person who is placed in the centre of the circle. Ask everyone to hold hands in the circle and then chose one person to stand in the middle and blow up a balloon. The people making up the circle are going to represent the expansion of the balloon. They

should begin by standing close to the person in the centre, as the balloon has not yet been blown up. As the blower begins to inflate the balloon, the circle should get bigger with the others moving away from the centre until the balloon blower claps their hands - everyone should fall to the floor, in other words, the balloon has burst!

This can be repeated with different people being chosen as the balloon blowers and may be helpful for focusing on reinforcing a sense of power and self-esteem in some of the less assertive members of the group.

Activities

7.1   Ranking Stress – Stress Cards

Prepare a copy of Worksheet 7.1 for each person: this shows a series of potentially stressful situations. Ask the group to rank these situations according to which they think is most stressful and why. Once they have done so, encourage a discussion of the responses in the group and consider whether stress is 'different' for each individual. Is stress person-specific? Why does something that stresses one person not make someone else feel stressed?

7.2   Stay Healthy! Statement Sorting

Give everyone a copy of worksheet 7.2 and ask them to cut out and then rank and sort the statements into what they feel are the most healthy options and the least healthy options. Once everyone has done so, ask the group to form pairs and compare their sequence with a partner and focus on the following questions: Do you agree on what constitutes a healthy lifestyle? Can you justify your ideas?

7.3   To Avoid Learning Stressors – Get Sorted!

Using worksheet 7.3, ask the group to read through the tips for 'organising yourself and your work'. Once again, they can place these in order of usefulness and then compare their ranking system with a partner. Do they agree? If not, why is this?

7.4   Stress Diary

This is a take-home task to be undertaken throughout the following week. Ask the group to keep a record of their stress levels over a one week period. They can make a tick against any of the statements that applied to them on each of the days of the week. Once they have completed this task they can then think carefully and reflect upon the following questions:

- Where are the highest and lowest stress points in your week?

- What is happening when you are most stressed?

- How can you (and others) alleviate these stressful times more effectively?

Feedback & Reflections

Ask the group to reflect upon what they have learnt in the session, posing the following questions:

- What was useful for you in this session?

- What might have made the session more useful for you?

- What have you learnt about yourself in today's session?

- What have you learnt about others?

- How will you use your knowledge and skills to help yourself and others in the future?

A Mindful Moment - The Stand-Up Game!

Ask the group to sit on chairs in a circle. Explain that for this exercise they are not allowed to talk or communicate with each other. They can only observe each other's actions and movements. Once everyone is settled, ask the group to stand up one at a time but no two people may stand up together! If two or more of the group stand up at the same time then they all have to start the task again.

7.1 Ranking Stress - Stress Cards

Read through the situation on the cards below.

Now rank these situations – which do you think is the most stressful and why?

Discuss your responses in the group and think about whether stress is different for each individual. Is stress person-specific? Why does something that stresses one person not make someone else feel stressed?

Changing your school or job	Having no money
Death of a close friend or member of the family	Having a row with your Mum or Dad or member of your family
Marriage or civil partnership	Leaving school
Getting divorced	Christmas
Pressure to take drugs	Pressure to have sex
Being bullied or intimidated by your boss or a teacher	Waiting in a queue for a bus or to pay for shopping
Going on holiday	Talking to your head teacher or Boss
Performing in front of an audience	Chatting to someone of the opposite sex
Driving a car	Tidying up
Thinking about school/work	Exams and assessments

7.2 Stay Healthy! Statement Sorting

Cut out these statements and then sort them into order, from the most healthy options to the least healthy options.

Compare your sequence with a partner. Do you agree on what constitutes a healthy lifestyle? Can you justify your ideas?

Taking regular exercise	Not eating junk food
Sleeping for 7 to 9 hours a night	Feeling happy and in control of your life
Eating a 'proper' breakfast	Enjoying hobbies
Eating fruit and vegetables	Having lots of money
Not smoking or taking drugs	Liking other people
Eating a low-fat diet	Being optimistic and positive
Not eating sweets	Eating at regular times
Having good friends	Going on holiday/taking a break
Having limited alcohol intake	Being able to relax
Being the 'right' weight for your height	Not getting anxious about things

7.3 To Avoid Learning Stressors - Get Sorted!

Read through the tips for organising yourself and your work. Cut out the cards and then place them in what you feel is their order of usefulness. Compare your ranking system with a partner. Do you agree? If not, why is this?

Keep a list of 'things to do' and tick them off as you go.	Prioritise your work and set dates to complete each piece – making sure these are realistic.	Make sure you sleep for at least 8 hours a night.
Know and use your learning styles and strengths.	Make up a study calendar every week.	Make sure you have a good place to work and concentrate.
Try to avoid using your mobile or looking at your facebook page when you are working.	Set time limits for each activity and try to keep to them.	Don't compare yourself to others who work differently or approach activities differently from you.
Set out all the things you need for your work the night before.	Eat, rest, play and work in a balanced way.	Plan regular breaks and rewards when you are working or studying.

7.4 Stress Diary

Keep a record of your stress levels over a one week period. Place a tick against any of the statements that applied to you on each of the days of the week.

	S	Sun	M	T	W	Th	F
Did you ...?							
Feel upset and moody?							
Get migraines/ headaches?							
Find it hard to concentrate?							
Sleep badly?							
Stop seeing friends?							
Get irritated about things?							
Feel very anxious?							
Take time off school?							
Feel fed up?							
Think that things are all your fault?							
Feel tired?							
Feel physically sick and wound up?							
Eat too much?							
Lose your appetite?							
Get annoyed with members of your family or friends?							
Feel that things are pointless?							
Feel that you just can't cope?							
Get very angry?							
Feel undermined by others?							
Lack confidence?							
Feel that you are worthless?							
Smoke/drink too much?							
Feel nervous?							
Keep your problems a secret?							
Argue with friends and family?							
Find it hard to make a decision?							
Feel frightened?							
Burst into tears?							
Feel dependent upon drugs?							
Get muscle ache?							
Feel sad?							
Feel 'butterflies' in your stomach?							
Forget things?							
Bite your nails?							
Get rashes?							
Feel a lump in your throat?							
Feel that your hands are sweating?							
Find yourself clenching your fists?							
Have nightmares, bad dreams?							
Feel isolated or lonely?							
Feel like hurting yourself?							

STOP, THINK & REFLECT

Where are the highest and lowest stress points in your week?

What is happening when you are most stressed?

How can you (and others) alleviate these stressful times more effectively?

Worksheet 7.4 Stress Diary

Session 8

Building Confidence & Self-Acceptance

Introduction & Aims

To start, reinforce the group rules as agreed in Session 1, and then outline the key aims for the session and briefly summarise the proposed activities.

The aims of this session are:

- To define the notion of confidence.

- To understand how appearance can be both a positive and negative element in developing our self confidence.

- To identify personal confidence levels.

- To recognize and analyse the four sources of confidence.

- To consider and discuss how people, places, situations and memories can all give and take away our confidence.

Icebreaker – A Question to Thought-Storm

Ask the question: 'What is confidence?'
Ask everyone to contribute their own ideas and definitions. These can be written on a whiteboard or flipchart and it may then be useful for the group, as a whole, to come up with their own agreed definition.

Students may also wish to focus upon some of the causes of their own levels of self-acceptance.

Warm-Up Game

The Balloon Game
This game aims to allow each student to feel part of the group whilst also encouraging a sense of power for the one who is placed in the centre of the circle. All of the students hold hands in the circle and one is chosen to stand in the middle and blow up a balloon. The circle here represents the expansion of the balloon, in other words, when they begin everyone is standing close to the student in the centre as the balloon has not been blown

Session 8 Building Confidence & Self-Acceptance

up. As the student blows into the balloon, the circle then gets bigger with the others moving away from the one in the centre until the balloon blower claps his/her hands and all the students are required to fall to the floor: the balloon has now burst! This can be repeated and it may be helpful for the teacher to particularly focus on reinforcing the sense of power and self-esteem for some of the less assertive members of the group.

Activities

8.1   Looking Good & Feeling Good

In this activity, the group are encouraged to explore and discuss a range of statements that are presented as myths and to try and discover the realities behind these statements. It is important to allow for sufficient time to discuss each statement in turn, as the resulting ideas and opinions will be rich and informative for the whole group.

8.2   How Confident are You?

For this activity, give the group worksheet 8.2 which contains a series of statements relating to confidence. Ask them to consider each statement in turn and to rank them in terms of how true each one is of them as individuals. They should score the statements using the scale from 1 to 5 as follows:1 = this is not me; 3 = this is sometimes me; 5 = this is always me.

The idea is to begin to identify levels of confidence and self-acceptance while also highlighting potential areas for future development.

8.3   What are Your Four Sources of Confidence?

Ask everyone to reflect upon their key sources of confidence and to record their ideas and responses on worksheet 8.3 under the following four headings:

* EXPERIENCE – Previous success will make you feel confident.

* ROLE MODELS – Positive people who are confident will inspire you.

* ENCOURAGEMENT – People who believe in you will make you feel confident.

* MANAGING FEELINGS – Your ability to manage stress and cope when it goes wrong will help you to feel confident.

Once everyone has completed the activity, it may be helpful to hold a whole group discussion about their responses and to consider any similarities and differences between them. For example, what are the key qualities of the positive people who inspire them? What do they have in common?

8.4   Givers & Takers

Encourage the group to consider and discuss how people, places, situations and memories can all give and take away our confidence. Ask them to record their examples on the worksheet – who gives them confidence and who and what takes it from them?

The aim of this activity is to enable reflection around the key positive qualities of those people in our lives who promote and foster our happiness and well-being as opposed to those who do not. It is important for young people to be able to identify those who are not helpful or encouraging and to understand how they can best be managed – or possibly even avoided!

8.5   I Like Me!

For this final thought-storming activity ask the group to reflect upon all the different things that they like about themselves and write or draw these in the spaces provided on the worksheet.

Feedback & Reflections

Ask the group to reflect upon what they have learnt in the session, posing the following questions:

- What was useful for you in this session?
- What might have made the session more useful for you?
- What have you learnt about yourself in today's session?
- What have you learnt about others?
- How will you use your knowledge and skills to help yourself and others in the future?

A Mindful Moment - Moving Mindfully

Explain to the group that they need spread out in the room and find themselves a space. Then they need to be very quiet and focus all of their attention on you.

Ask the group to pay attention to all the movements you make and to try to copy these as closely as they possibly can. Actions could include the following:

- Do a one-legged squat.
- Lie down and breathe deeply.
- Make a star shape.
- Raise both arms slowly above your head.

8.1 Looking Good & Feeling Good

Explore these myths and try to discover the realities that lie behind them.

Myth	Reality
How you look is what really matters.	
If you look like your friends you will feel happy.	
If you are a rich, beautiful and famous celebrity you will be happy.	
Girls care more about how they look than boys do.	

8.2 How Confident are You?

Think about the following statements and whether they apply to you, then rate the following statements on the scale from 1 to 5.

1 = this is not me 3 = this is sometimes me 5 = this is always me

I feel relaxed	1	2	3	4	5
I feel secure	1	2	3	4	5
I believe in myself	1	2	3	4	5
I don't think others are always better than me	1	2	3	4	5
I set realistic goals	1	2	3	4	5
I do as well as I can	1	2	3	4	5
I don't behave in an aggressive way or show off when I feel insecure	1	2	3	4	5
I act confident even if I don't feel like it	1	2	3	4	5
My level of self-esteem is good	1	2	3	4	5
I don't always worry about what others think	1	2	3	4	5
I tend to achieve what I want	1	2	3	4	5

8.3 What are Your Four Sources of Confidence?

Think about your sources of confidence and record them under the headings on the chart below.

1. EXPERIENCE Previous success will make you feel confident.
2. ROLE MODELS Positive people who are confident will inspire you.
3. ENCOURAGEMENT People who believe in you will make you feel confident.
4. MANAGING FEELINGS Your ability to manage stress and cope when it goes wrong will help you to feel confident.

8.4 Givers & Takers

People, places, situations and memories can all give and take away our confidence. Think about who gives you confidence and who and what takes it from you? Record your answers in the table below.

CONFIDENCE GIVERS	CONFIDENCE TAKERS

Stop, Think & Reflect

How can you reduce the number of confidence takers in your life?

What can you do? Draw up a list of strategies to avoid the confidence takers.

8.5 I Like Me!

I like myself because…

I like myself because…

I like myself because…

I like myself because…

Accept 4 Respect Yourself

I like myself because…

I like myself because…

I like myself because…

I like myself because…

Signed _____ Date _____

Session 9
Positive Comments

Introduction 4 Aims

To start, reinforce the group rules as agreed in Session 1, and then outline the key aims for the session and briefly summarise the proposed activities.

The aims of this session are:

- To understand the importance of developing and maintaining a positive attitude and outlook.
- To understand how positive comments and empathy can support others in developing and maintain a positive stance.
- To identify and celebrate positive traits.
- To be able to understand how showing gratitude is a key to greater happiness and is also a very good happy habit to develop.

Icebreaker – A Question to Thought-Storm

Ask the question: 'What does the word "positive" mean to you?'
Ask everyone to contribute their own ideas and definitions. These can be written on a whiteboard or flipchart and it may then be useful for the group, as a whole, to come up with their own agreed definition. The group may wish to also focus upon some of the causes of the positive feelings that they are currently experiencing in their lives.

Warm-Up Game

Being Leaders
Ask one person to leave the room while the others agree who will be the leader. When the person returns from outside the chosen leader should begin to make a movement which all the others in the group should follow and copy. The leader then changes to a different movement and everyone else in the group again copies what they are doing. The person who left the room must try to spot the leader. Once the leader has been spotted, they then leave the room, someone else can be chosen as the leader.

Activities

9.1 Empathetic words

Ask the group to consider how sometimes it can be quite hard to find the words needed to empathise with someone else. Ask them to consider the statements on worksheet 9.1 and to try to think what they would say in order to show empathy for each person involved. They can write their responses in the speech bubbles provided.

9.2 Positive Remarks

This activity reinforces the importance of being positive about yourself and about the people you meet. This attitude can help us to succeed and achieve our goals. Being able to acknowledge, value and praise the efforts and strengths of others will also have a knock-on effect for the recipients in terms of ensuring that they also feel positive about themselves!

Organise the group into a seated circle and encourage them, in turn, to follow the following instructions:

Make a positive remark about:
   a. The person on your left

   b. The person on your right

   c. The person opposite you

The comments can be written in the boxes on worksheet 9.2 and the recipients of the comments can then write their response in the response box.

9.3 What are Your Positive Traits?

Give each person a copy of worksheet 9.3 which contains a list of positive traits. Ask them to read through these and to place a tick against those traits that they feel they possess. Now ask people to think about other positive traits that they have and add these to the list.

9.4 Giving Credit Where it's Due!

Make a List! Ask everyone to think of all the people who have helped and supported them in their lives. On worksheet 9.4 write a list of credits, identifying what the person did to help them and why they are so grateful. Showing gratitude in this way is a key to greater happiness and is also a very good 'happy habit' to develop. It is also very important in terms of showing gratitude: valuing others and showing them that the good things that they have done should and will produce positive feelings and emotions – both in the giver and the recipient.

Feedback & Reflections

Ask the group to reflect upon what they have learnt in the session, posing the following questions:

- What was useful for you in this session?
- What might have made the session more useful for you?
- What have you learnt about yourself in today's session?
- What have you learnt about others?
- How will you use your knowledge and skills to help yourself and others in the future?

A Mindful Moment - Breathing Mindfully to Relax

Ask everyone to sit in a comfortable position, and to become aware of their posture, either sitting on a cushion on the floor or on a chair. Then close their eyes so that they can really focus on this activity.

Now introduce this mindful breathing exercise with the following script:

Please now bring your attention to your breathing. You can focus on the breath as it enters and leaves your nose, noticing how the air feels cool coming in and slightly warmer leaving your nose. Or you may choose to focus on the breath at your belly, feeling it rise with the in-breath and fall with the out-breath. Stay focused, as much you can, on your breath without trying to control it in any way. Notice the air as it enters and as it leaves, entering and leaving. If your mind wanders, that's fine. Just bring your attention back to the in-breath and the out-breath. Breathing in and breathing out. Your mind will naturally wander off and get lost in thoughts. That's okay. It's just what minds do. Your job is to gently bring your attention back to the breath each time you notice that your mind has wandered. You may tell yourself 'well done' for noticing and then continue to focus on your breath.

(Adapted from Semple & Lee, 2008, p.76.)

Session 9 Positive Comments

9.1 Empathetic Words

Sometimes it can be quite hard to find the words needed to empathise with someone else. Look at the following statements and try to think what you would say in order to show empathy for each person. Write your response in the speech bubbles.

'I'm so rubbish at writing. I may as well not even try. I feel so dumb!'

'My dad has grounded me for smoking. It's so unfair when he smokes himself.'

'I'm so ugly. I feel that I need plastic surgery or I'll never get a girlfriend.'

'That teacher has just got it in for me. I keep getting into trouble and it's not my fault. She just wants me out.'

'My mum keeps saying how disappointed she is in me for getting excluded. She says I'm bad, I feel so fed up, and it's all useless.'

9.2 Positive Remarks

Look Positive!	Speak Positive!	Act Positive!

It is important to be positive about yourself and about the people you meet. Your attitude will help you to succeed and achieve your goals. You will also ensure that others feel positive about themselves!

When you are seated in a circle, make a positive remark about:

- The person on your left
- The person on your right
- The person opposite you

Write your comment in the box and then ask each person to write their reply in the response box.

Positive Comment	Response
a.	
b.	
c.	

Questions to discuss and think about:

- How did each person respond to receiving a compliment? For example, were they smiling, happy, fidgeting, looking away, embarrassed?
- What is a good response to receiving a positive compliment?
- What would not be a good response and why?

9.3 What are Your Positive Traits?

Read through the list of positive traits in the list below. Tick the ones that describe you!
Can you add any more positive traits that you have?

Kind	Insightful	Sensitive
Intelligent	Funny	Organised
Hardworking	Patient	Selfless
Loyal	Realistic	Practical
Attractive	Honest	Mature
Down-to-earth	Generous	Focused
Goofy	Modest	Courteous
Creative	Serious	Grateful
Accepting	Independent	Open-minded
Strong	Trusting	Positive
Friendly	Resilient	Responsible
Flexible	Cheerful	Cooperative
Nurturing	Self-directed	Frugal
Thoughtful	Reliable	Tolerant
Confident	Relaxed	Innovative
Optimistic	Listener	Balanced
Respectful	Brave	Motivated
Determined	Decisive	Humble
Skilled	Enthusiastic	
Helpful	Forgiving	

9.4 Giving Credit Where it's Due!

Make Your list!

Think of all the people who have helped and supported you. Write a list of credits, identifying what they did to help you and why you are so grateful to them.

Name of person	What they did to support or help me

Session 10
Healthy Habits

Introduction & Aims

To start, reinforce the group rules as agreed in Session 1, and then outline the key aims for the session and briefly summarise the proposed activities.

The aims of this session are:

- To understand and define a habit and to be able to distinguish between healthy and unhealthy habits.

- To clarify the most and least healthy leisure activities that people engage in and consider how they might make their leisure time more productive and enjoyable.

- To understand the psychological and mental benefits of exercise as including better overall well-being, better body image, increased self-esteem and confidence, lower anxiety, depression and stress levels.

- To understand the physical benefits of exercise which include a reduction in obesity, cardiovascular disease, heart disease, strokes, diabetes (type 2), high blood pressure and some cancers.

- To understand the need to take personal responsibility for keeping healthy.

Icebreaker – A Question to Thought-Storm

Ask the question: 'What is a habit?'
Ask everyone to contribute their own ideas and definitions. These can be written on a whiteboard or flipchart and it may then be useful for the group, as a whole, to come up with their own agreed definition.

The group may wish to also focus upon some of their own habits and distinguish between those that are healthy and those that are unhealthy. They can also discuss whether it is possible and, indeed, a good thing to be able to develop healthier habits in order to further enhance our well-being.

Session 10 Healthy Habits

Warm-Up Game

Letterbox

This is a fast moving game in which people are required to listen carefully and be alert and ready for action. Print the letters of the alphabet on cards and use the complete alphabet to ensure that the initials of each group member is included. Place the cards in a box or bag.

Ask the group to sit in the circle and start by placing an object in the centre of the circle. Now select a letter card from the box and say: 'Anyone whose name begins with …?' Anyone who fits into that category must stand up and run around the circle in a clockwise direction. When they arrive back at their seats they must enter the circle and attempt to pick up the object in the middle. The person who picks up the object pulls the next letter from the box and calls it out.

You will need to make sure that the letters are not returned to the box after each turn. The person who calls out the letters can also decide how the others will move around the outside of the circle, for example, hop, crawl, skip, jump, etc.

Activities

10.1   Keep Healthy – Healthy Options

Give each person a copy of worksheet 10.1 which contains a list of activities. Ask them to cut out these cards and then sort them into order in terms of the most healthy options and least healthy options. Once everyone has done so, discuss in the group any similarities and differences in people's responses.

10.2   Leisure Activities

Ask the group to focus on and think about their leisure activities. They can list these on the chart on worksheet 10.2. Next, rank each activity – placing the most important one first and the least important last. Finally, everyone should look at the list of activities and identify the most and least healthy activities and consider how they might make their leisure time more productive and enjoyable.

10.3 My Exercise Diary

Discuss among the group how the psychological and mental benefits of exercise include better overall well-being, better body image, increased self-esteem and confidence, lower anxiety, depression and stress levels. Physical benefits include a reduction in obesity, cardiovascular disease, heart disease, strokes, diabetes (type 2), high blood pressure and some cancers.

In this activity, therefore, the group are encouraged to keep on moving! Encourage everyone to find out what exercise suits and motivates them: dance, gym, football, etc. Then they can work out a weekly timetable and complete the exercise diary on the worksheet.

10.4 Exercise Mind Map

To end, ask the group to thought-storm, working together to identify as many different physical activities as possible that could help them to keep fit, for example skipping, judo, trampolining, taekwondo, swimming, kickboxing, surfing, jazz, ballet. They can create a mind map of their ideas on worksheet 10.4.

Feedback 4 Reflections

Ask the group to reflect upon what they have learnt in the session, posing the following questions:

- What was useful for you in this session?
- What might have made the session more useful for you?
- What have you learnt about yourself in today's session?
- What have you learnt about others?
- How will you use your knowledge and skills to help yourself and others in the future?

A Mindful Moment - Thought-Watching at the March!

This exercise supports the group in watching their thoughts without believing them or taking them personally. It supports the de-personalisation process which, in turn, facilitates a less busy and judgemental mindset!

Ask everyone to sit in chairs or lie on the floor, anchor their attention on their breathing, and then begin to watch their thoughts go by as if they were watching a march proceeding along their high street. Encourage them to notice that some thoughts are loud and brightly dressed, while other thoughts are shy and lurk in the background, and still others come back again and again.

Next, ask everyone to notice when they start to march along with the other participants (in other words, when they are lost in thought). When this happens, encourage people to try to return to the path and simply watch their thoughts pass by in the march.

10.1 Keep Healthy - Healthy Options

Cut out these cards showing different activities and then sort them into order in terms of the most healthy options and least healthy options.

Now compare your sequence with other people.

Do you agree on what constitutes a healthy lifestyle? Can you justify your sequence?

Taking regular exercise	Not eating junk food
Going to lots of parties	Unprotected sex
Sleeping for 7-9 hours a night	Feeling happy
Low self-esteem	Feeling confident
Eating a 'proper' breakfast	Enjoying hobbies
Eating fruit and vegetables	Having lots of money
Not smoking or taking drugs	Liking other people
Eating a high fat diet	Being optimistic
Not eating sweets or too much sugar	Eating at regular times
Having good friends	Going on holiday
Eating fibre each day	Being able to relax
A low fat diet	A high fat diet
Being the 'right' weight for your height	Not getting anxious about things

10.2 Leisure Activities

List your leisure activities on the chart below.

Now rank each one – placing the most important one first and the least important last. Then identify the most and least healthy activities and consider how you might make your leisure time more productive and enjoyable.

Compare your responses with a friend and highlight any similarities and differences.

Leisure Activity	Rank order?	Healthy or Not healthy?

10.3 My Exercise Diary

The psychological and mental benefits of exercise include better overall well-being, better body image, increased self-esteem and confidence, lower anxiety, depression and stress levels. Physical benefits include a reduction in obesity, cardiovascular disease, heart disease, strokes, diabetes (type 2), high blood pressure and some cancers.

SO KEEP ON MOVING!

Find out what exercise suits you and motivates you: it could be dance, gym, or football. Now work out a weekly timetable and complete the exercise diary.

	My exercise of choice	Time I spent on this	Feelings during exercise	Feelings after exercise
Monday				
Tuesday				
Wednesday				
Thursday				
Friday				
Saturday				
Sunday				

10.4 Exercise Mind Map

Thought-storm!

Work together to identify as many different physical activities that could help you keep fit, for example skipping, judo, trampolining, taekwondo, swimming, kickboxing, surfing, jazz, ballet, etc. etc. Create a mind map of this list below.

Exercise
Mind Map

Effective Thinking Part 1

Introduction & Aims

To start, reinforce the group rules as agreed in Session 1, and then outline the key aims for the session and briefly summarise the proposed activities.

The aims of this session are:

- To clarify and define ineffective thinking and the need to be able to reframe negative automatic thoughts which are not helpful to us.

- To understand the idea that thoughts, feelings and behaviours are all connected, and how the CBT approach breaks a particular problem into three smaller parts.

- To know that core beliefs are the strong, enduring ideas that we may have about ourselves and how this kind of belief system gives rise to rules, demands or assumptions which in turn produce automatic thoughts.

- To identify and analyse our own core beliefs.

- To develop skills in reframing ineffective thoughts (NATs).

Icebreaker - A Question to Thought-Storm

Ask question: 'What is ineffective thinking?'
Ask everyone to contribute their own ideas and definitions. These can be written on a whiteboard or flipchart and it may then be useful for the group, as a whole, to come up with their own agreed definition.

The group may wish to also focus upon some of the negative thoughts that they are currently trying to manage or finding problematic. What are they currently doing in order to be able to adjust such thoughts? Are they aware of the link between negative thoughts and subsequent feelings and behaviours?

Warm-Up Game

Hesitation
Begin by asking the group to sit in a circle, then choose a category such as pop stars, sport stars, items of clothing, computer games or sandwich fillings. Select one of the group to begin the game. They must name an item that fits within the chosen category and then everyone in the circle should clap twice in unison. Next, the person to their left names another item within the category. Everyone claps twice again and the activity proceeds

around the circle. An item is not allowed to be named twice and if someone hesitates after the clapping, the group should clap four more times and shout 'Hesitation!'. That person then has to select a new category and the game continues. It may be useful to thought-storm possible categories and their contents before beginning the game in order to provide the group with some ideas to work from.

Activities

11.1   What is Cognitive Behaviour Therapy (CBT)?

Worksheet 11.1 provides the group members with an outline of the basic premise of CBT – the idea that thoughts, feelings and behaviours are all connected.

The CBT approach breaks any particular problem into three smaller parts:

- **A:** the **activating event** is often referred to as the 'trigger' – the thing that causes you to engage in the negative thinking.

- **B:** this represents these negative **beliefs**, which can include thoughts, rules and demands, and the meanings, an individual attaches to both external and internal events.

- **C:** the **consequences**, or emotions, and the behaviours and physical sensations accompanying these different emotions. It is important to highlight and discuss with the group how the way that they think about a problem can affect how they feel physically and emotionally. It can also alter what they do about it. This is why the key aim for CBT is to break the negative, vicious cycle that some people may find themselves in. For example, if you think that you will get your work wrong you feel angry, and then you do not give it a try in case it is wrong.

11.2   Who Am I? My Core Beliefs

In this activity the group members have to think about how they would describe themselves. Core beliefs are the strong, enduring ideas that we may have about ourselves. This kind of belief system gives rise to rules, demands or assumptions, which in turn produce automatic thoughts. Core beliefs generally fall into three main categories: beliefs about yourself; beliefs about other people in the world; beliefs that are either positive or negative. What is important is to identify our core beliefs and to also consider why these may or may not be unhelpful. In this way we can begin to identify negative automatic thoughts (NATs).

11.3   Negative Automatic Thoughts – NATs!

This two-part activity provides young people, through the use of worksheet 11.3a, with a visual chart to show the development of negative automatic thinking, and also with a template on worksheet 11.3b to chart one of their own negative automatic thoughts. The idea here is to reinforce the links between thoughts, feelings and behaviours for each individual person.

Some of the thoughts that people may hold about themselves could include the following:

- I always look ugly.

- I don't understand this work.

- He thinks I'm stupid and an idiot.

- She gave me a nasty look.

- I'm just such a useless person.

- I can't do that and I'll never be able to do it like other people can.

11.4   NATs – Breaking the Cycle!

When working with young people in identifying such faulty thinking, the main aim is to encourage them to break the negative cycle.

These NATs can arise from a number of errors in our thinking. We need to challenge our negative thoughts and always check out the evidence to discover how true these thoughts actually are and how we can change negative thoughts into more balanced ones. Ask the group to use the template on worksheet 11.4 have a go at reframing a series of NATs. Worksheet 11.4 shows one done for them:

NAT: *I'm terrible at keeping in touch with friends*
Evidence: I often go weeks without speaking to some of my friends.

I may not talk to my oldest friends as much as I would like, but they are still my oldest friends for a reason!
And when we do get together it's like we've never been apart!

Feedback & Reflections

Ask the group to reflect upon what they have learnt in the session, posing the following questions:

- What was useful for you in this session?

- What might have made the session more useful for you?

- What have you learnt about yourself in today's session?

- What have you learnt about others?

- How will you use your knowledge and skills to help yourself and others in the future?

A Mindful Moment – The Hand Game

Ask everyone to join you sitting around a table. Now ask each person to place their hands on the table, with the hand of the person next to them in the space between their hands.

Now explain the rules: when one person taps their hand on the table, the next person (starting clockwise) taps their hand … and so on. If someone taps their hand at the wrong time, you must remove one of their hands from the table. If a person taps their hand twice on the table, the direction of the tap reverses. The winner is the person with one hand left on the table.

11.1 What is Cognitive Behavioural Therapy (CBT)?

CBT is a set of tools to help you deal with problems and find the best solutions.

Looking at the links between …

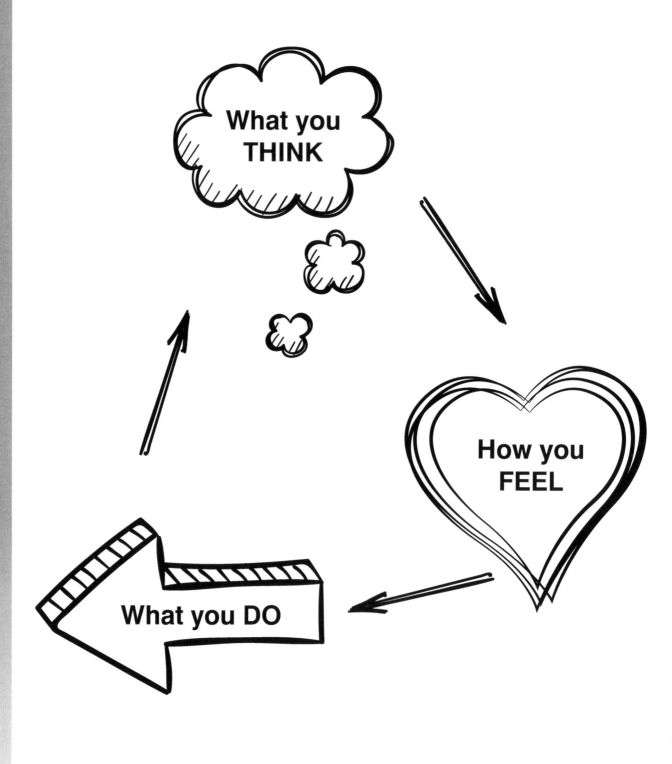

11.2 Who am I? My Core Beliefs

How would you describe yourself, what are you like?

1..

2..

3..

4..

5..

6..

7..

8..

9..

10..

11..

12..

13..

14..

15..

16..

17..

18..

19..

20..

11.3a Negative Automatic Thoughts - NATs!

Confirms negative thoughts
(I'm terrible at keeping in touch with friends)

Negative thought
(I'm terrible at keeping in touch with friends)

Causes you to behave in a certain way
(Not getting in contact with friends)

Makes you feel worried and unsure
(I must be a terrible friend, why would anyone want to hear from me?)

Produces uncomfortable feelings
(I'm not sure I want to contact my friends now, I feel too awkward)

11.3b The Negative Cycle

Try and have a go yourself...

Confirms negative thoughts

Negative thought

Makes you feel worried and unsure

Causes you to behave in a certain way

Produces uncomfortable feelings

11.4 NATs - Breaking the Cycle!

We need to challenge our negative thoughts and always check out the evidence behind them to discover how true these thoughts actually are and how can we change negative thoughts into more balanced ones.

Have a go at reframing some NATs and breaking the cycle! The first one is done for you.

1.   **I'm terrible at keeping in touch with friends.**

   Evidence: I often go weeks without speaking to some of my friends.

   I may not talk to my oldest friends as much as I would like, but they are still my oldest friends for a reason! And when we do get together it's like we've never been apart!

2.   **I always get left out.**

   Evidence:

3.   **I can't do this activity.**

   Evidence:

4.   **I never look as good as my mates.**

   Evidence:

5.   **My work is never as good as the others.**

   Evidence:

6.   **I always misbehave.**
   Evidence:

Session 12
Effective Thinking Part 2

Introduction & Aims

To start, reinforce the group rules as agreed in Session 1, and then outline the key aims for the session and briefly summarise the proposed activities.

The aims of this session are:

- Defining the qualities of a positive person.
- Recognising and understanding the six kinds of faulty thinking.
- Understanding how interventions for developing new and more positive belief systems (behavioural experiments) and for challenging these negative automatic thoughts can test the evidence.
- Knowing how to use distraction as a tool for controlling thoughts and trying out a range of these strategies.

Icebreaker – A Question to Thought-Storm

Ask the question: 'What are the qualities or characteristics of a positive person?'
Ask everyone to contribute their own ideas and definitions. These can be written on a whiteboard or flipchart and it may then be useful for the group, as a whole, to come up with their own agreed list of qualities and attributes.

The group may wish to also focus upon some of their own attributes and identify some of the times when they have engaged in reframing and replacing negative automatic thoughts with more effective ones.

Warm-Up Game

Changes
Ask everyone to sit in a circle and then ask for a volunteer to leave the room. Once the person has left, choose two people to swap places and then ask the volunteer to come back in. After looking around carefully, they have to guess what has changed. Once they have done so, choose someone else to leave the room for the next round. This activity can be varied in many different ways. For example, group members could swap jumpers or other articles of clothing, or some may take off jackets, jumpers or shoes.

The aim of this game is not just to have fun but also to focus on the importance of really looking at and observing people in order to see how they are acting and feeling.

Activities

12.1 Six Kinds of Faulty Thinking! Are YOU Guilty?

There are six kinds of faulty thinking as outlined on worksheet 12.1. Ask everyone to read through each of these and try to identify any that they themselves have engaged in. When working with young people, it is important to allow them time to consider the effects that these NATs can have on their overall well-being prior to them beginning to implement some changes.

12.2 Thought Detective!

One of the most helpful interventions for developing new and more positive belief systems, and for challenging these negative automatic thoughts, is to test the evidence. Using Worksheet 12.2a and 12.2b ask the group to engage in the following questioning process:

1. What is the evidence for this thought?

2. What is the evidence against this thought?

3. What would my best friend say if they heard my thought?

4. What would my teacher say if he heard my thought?

5. What would my parents or carers say if they heard my thought?

6. What would I say to my best friend if s/he had this same thought?

7. Am I making mistakes? For example, blowing it up out of proportion, forgetting my strengths or good points, self-blaming or predicting failure, or thinking that I can mind-read what others are thinking?

This kind of strategy is particularly useful in terms of reinforcing the need to gather accurate evidence. What we believe about ourselves is not always true. It is not how others always see us and these types of belief need to be challenged in this way. Using this sort of questioning process, and gathering evidence in this format, is a particularly positive strategy for beginning to identify and challenge the unhelpful beliefs that young people may carry.

12.3 Controlling Thoughts Using Distraction!

Explain to the group that they can control their thoughts by thinking of something else, for example, they could:

* Describe in detail what they see around them in order to feel calmer.

* Attempt to name all of their favourite bands.

* Use self-talk techniques and repeat a positive coping message until the negative automatic thought has gone.

* 'Bin' the thoughts by writing them down and then screwing them up and putting them into the wastepaper bin – symbolically eradicating these negative thoughts.

* Keep a positive diary in order to record positive automatic thoughts (PATs) that may occur during the day, and also engage in realistic goal-setting which involves practice.

Worksheet 12.3 explains how this can work and summarises these strategies. Ask the group members to discuss with a partner any of the strategies they currently use and any others they might try in the future.

When working with young people, to help them to learn and develop these skills it is important to encourage them to set appropriate targets. They need to be reminded that it is difficult to move forwards unless we set realistic goals for ourselves. These goals should be broken down into small, achievable steps and the ultimate goal continually focused upon. Setting targets allows us to visualise where we want to be in the future: if we feel that we have nowhere to go, or nothing to move towards, then ultimately we will not be able to affect the changes we desire.

12.4 Test It! My Most Frequent Negative Thought
In this activity, explain to the group members that they are going to design their own behavioural experiment in order to test one of the negative automatic thoughts they have most frequently.

First, they need to identify a negative thought that they have often. Next, ask them to rate how strongly they believe this on a scale from 1 to 10. Now they must come up with a way of testing whether or not their thought is true, and plan when they will carry out their experiment. Once they have done so, they need to feedback about what they found out – were they right? Was their thought true? How do they feel about it now?

Feedback & Reflections

Ask the group to reflect upon what they have learnt in the session, posing the following questions:

- What was useful for you in this session?
- What might have made the session more useful for you?
- What have you learnt about yourself in today's session?
- What have you learnt about others?
- How will you use your knowledge and skills to help yourself and others in the future?

A Mindful Moment - Valuing Exercise

Ask everyone to sit in a circle and to take turns to each state one thing that they value about the others in the group. For example, 'I value the way you help me when I'm finding the maths difficult', or 'I really like it when you include me in your group', or 'I value you as a friend'.

Encourage the group to affirm these connections and reinforce how important it is for all of us to be seen, acknowledged and loved.

Finally, ask the group to reflect upon the following question: How does being valued make them feel?

12.1 Six Kinds of Faulty Thinking! Are YOU Guilty?

There are six kinds of faulty thinking … do any of these sound familiar to you?

1. DOING DOWN!

- Only focusing on negatives.
- Only seeing the bad bit in something that was good overall.
- Not counting a positive, for example: 'She only wants to go out with me because she can't find anyone else.'

2. BLOWING UP OUT OF PROPORTION!

- Making things worse than they are.
- It's all or nothing, for example, 'I only got 88% and not 100% – it's not good enough!'
- Magnifying the problem, for example, 'I got the answer wrong and everyone in the class laughed at me!' Or, 'It's a catastrophe! I'll never get over it!'

3. PREDICTING FAILURE!

- Mind-reading to predict failure, for example, 'I bet they are all laughing at me!' Or, 'I know he hates me!'
- Fortune-telling – knowing you will fail, for example, 'I know I won't be able to do that work' Or, 'I know they won't like me.'

4. OVER-EMOTIONAL THOUGHTS!

- With this faulty thinking our emotions become very strong and cloud the way we think and understand things.
- Because we feel bad we presume everything is bad – the emotions take over!
- We attach negative labels to ourselves, for example, 'I'm rubbish/stupid/a loser.'

5. SETTING YOURSELF UP!

- Setting targets too high and setting yourself up to fail.
- 'I should …', 'I must …', 'I can't …', 'I want …', 'I shouldn't …'
- Creating standards that are impossible to achieve.

6. BLAMING YOURSELF

- Everything that goes wrong/is wrong is your fault – even stuff you have no control over! 'I got into my car and it broke down!' Or, 'I turned on the computer and it crashed!'

12.2a Thought Detective! Part 1

Test your thoughts by finding the EVIDENCE!

DAY & TIME	THOUGHT Rate how much you believe it, 1-10 (10=totally)	EVIDENCE FOR the thought	EVIDENCE AGAINST the thought
1			
2			
3			
4			

12.2b Thought Detective! Part 2

Test your thoughts by finding the EVIDENCE!

THOUGHT	What would my best friend say to me?	What would I say to my best friend if they had this thought?	How much do I believe this thought now? 1-10 (10 = totally)
1			
2			
3			
4			

12.3 Controlling Thoughts Using Distraction!

Facts

- We listen to our thoughts a lot.

- We often accept negative thoughts as 'the truth' without really challenging them.

- These thoughts can become louder and it becomes harder to hear the positive thoughts.

- The more we listen to them, the more uncomfortable and down we feel and the less we do – it's a TRAP!!

The Solution: Distraction

- Helps you take your mind off the negative thoughts.

- Helps you take CONTROL of your thoughts by thinking of something else.

- You DROWN OUT those negative thoughts by ensuring your mind does what YOU want it to!

Strategies to Try

- Describing what you see
- Puzzle it out!
- Get absorbed
- Self-talking
- Top talk

- Worry box
- Turn it down!
- Test it!
- Bin them!

Which of these strategies do you use now?

Which ones might you try in the future?

Discuss with a partner.

12.4 Test It! My Most Frequent Negative Thought

1. Identify the negative thought you have most often.

_____

2. Scale It
   Mark out of 10 for how strongly you believe this thought to be true (0 = not strongly; 5 = quite strongly; 10 = extremely strongly)

   0   1   2   3   4   5   6   7   8   9   10

3. Design an Experiment
   What test could you set up to see if your thought is true?

4. When will you do this?

5. If you think your negative thought is true, what do you think will happen?

AFTERWARDS...

- What DID happen when you tested your thought?

_____

- How strongly do you believe your thought now?

_____

Session 13
Mindful Moments

Introduction & Aims

To start, reinforce the group rules as agreed in Session 1, and then outline the key aims for the session and briefly summarise the proposed activities.

The aims of this session are:

- To understand what mindfulness is and how it can impact positively upon our well-being.

- To define mindfulness.

- To explain its key benefits.

- To engage in a range of activities and recognise how and when these can be used in other contexts such as home.

The key aim of this session is to reinforce the practice of mindfulness by devoting a whole session to these activities and also encouraging young people to keep a daily log or diary of mindfulness activities which they will make use of both at school and at home. The focus is on reinforcing just how useful mindfulness is in reducing anxiety and in slowing down and calming our over-busy minds. These tools can be used by everyone throughout their lives to support emotional and mental well-being.

You may find it helpful to recap the definitions and also the purpose of the practice of mindfulness prior to engaging in the activities. The following script can be used when working with your group:

Mindfulness exercises allow you to be able to identify, tolerate and reduce difficult, painful and even frightening thoughts, feelings and sensations. Mindfulness gives you back some sense of mastery over your thoughts and feelings. Rather than having the sense that you are being pushed around by your feelings and thoughts you learn to be able to have some control over them. This is very important as we know that people who feel in control of themselves and their lives are far less likely to experience high levels of anxiety.

The following definitions of mindfulness can help us to understand this process. Mindfulness can be described as:

- The awareness that emerges through paying attention on purpose, in the present moment, and non-judgmentally to the unfolding of experience moment to moment. (Kabat-Zinn, 2003)

- The non-judgmental observation of the on-going stream of internal and external stimuli as they arise. (Baer, 2003)

- Keeping one's complete attention to the experience on a moment to moment basis. (Martlett & Kristeller, 1999)

Put simply, mindfulness is as simple as becoming aware of your here-and-now experience, both internally and in the external world around you. It gives you a space in the present moment to be able to more safely deal with the distressing and painful memories of things that might have happened to you in the past. It also allows you to look at and plan for the future, even when you might have fearful thoughts about things that haven't yet happened, from a secure position of knowing that you are in the present moment.

Icebreaker - A Question to Thought-Storm

Ask the question: 'What are the qualities of a mindful person?'
Ask everyone to contribute their own ideas and definitions. These can be written on a whiteboard or flipchart and it may then be useful for the group, as a whole, to come up with their own agreed list of qualities and attributes.

Ask the group to focus on some of their own attributes and identify some of the times when they have engaged in mindful behaviours and activities and the impact that these had on their well-being in general.

Warm-Up

Game Racing Whispers
Organise everyone into two groups. Each group must now stand in a line, one behind the other, with an arm's length of space between each person. This is to ensure that only the people at the front of each line are able to hear the whispered message. Now sit on a chair some distance from the two groups and explain that you are going to whisper an action to the two people at the front of the lines. They must then whisper the action to the second person and so on. Once the whisper has reached the last person, they have to run up to the front and perform the action for you. You can award points for how close the action is to the original whisper. The people who performed the actions can go to the front of the line and the process is then repeated.

The idea is to reinforce the importance of communicating clearly and also of listening carefully when receiving a message.

Activities

13.1   What is Mindfulness all About?
Worksheet 13.1 can be given to the group at the start of the session in order to reinforce the session aims and introduction. This provides a definition of mindfulness and also a simple technique to try, as well as links to a mindfulness app. Discuss the definition and the technique with the group.

13.2 Mindful Activity 1: Listen to the Sounds

For this first activity ask the group to sit comfortably on a chair or the carpet and close their eyes. Use the script on Worksheet 13.2 and encourage the group to focus on the sounds that they can hear.

13.3 Mindful Activity 2: Mindful Music

Choose a piece of music to play to the group – preferably one which most of them will like. Explain to the group that they should not think about it – but to simply listen. They can then be asked to breathe deeply and slowly to absorb the experience.

13.4 Mindful Activity 3: My Peaceful Place

Using Worksheet 13.4, read the 'Peaceful Place' script to the group and encourage everyone to try to return to their 'peaceful place' whenever they feel upset or stressed.

13.5 Mindful Homework Tasks & Mindfulness Activity Record

Give everyone worksheet 13.5a, which outlines some mindfulness homework tasks, as well as worksheet 13.5b, a record sheet that they can use to track their engagement in these activities on a weekly basis. Explain that they can use the mindfulness activities explored in the group, as well as those on the worksheet, when they get home. Group members can use the record sheet to chart the activities they have tried, when they tried them, how they felt and what thoughts they had. They could also give the activities a score out of 10.

Feedback & Reflections

Ask the group to reflect upon what they have learnt in the session, posing the following questions:

- What was useful for you in this session?
- What might have made the session more useful for you?
- What have you learnt about yourself in today's session?
- What have you learnt about others?
- How will you use your knowledge and skills to help yourself and others in the future?

A Final Mindful Moment – Wishing You Well!

Ask everyone to sit in a circle and then turn to the people either side and tell them the good things they wish for one another. For example:

- I hope that you are happy in your life
- I hope you have good and loyal friends
- I hope you don't have big problems in your life
- I hope that you are full of energy and successful.

Encourage group members to notice how others' good wishes make them feel and to respond to these good wishes with similar ones of their own. Why do they think it is so important to have such feelings? What might life be like without them?

Session 13 Mindful Moments

13.1 What is Mindfulness all About?

A Definition

Mindfulness is a way of paying attention to the present moment. When we're mindful we become more aware of our thoughts and feelings and better able to manage them.

Being mindful can boost our concentration, improve our relationships and help with stress or depression. It can even have a positive effect on physical problems like chronic pain.

Anyone can learn to be mindful. It's simple, you can do it anywhere, and the results can be life-changing.

A Technique to Try: The Waterfall

Sometimes feelings and thoughts are uncomfortable and too difficult to focus on. Instead of getting caught up in thoughts or reacting to the negative feelings, picture yourself standing behind a waterfall of negative thoughts and feelings, allowing them to be there without reacting to them. See those thoughts and feelings as part of you but not as being all that you are.

(Adapted from Segal, Williams & Teasdale 2002, pp.250–51.)

Take 10 minutes each day to do a simple mindfulness meditation

Many of us spend much of our time focused either on the past or on the future, paying very little attention to what is happening right now.

Being mindful involves staying in the moment, spending more time noticing what's going on both inside ourselves and in our surroundings. Rather than trying to change anything, it involves accepting the way that things are, for better or for worse.

You can follow a free 10-day daily guided meditation on the Headspace website:
www.getsomeheadspace.com

You can also download the free Headspace app here:
http://www.getsomeheadspace.com/shop/headspace-meditation-app.aspx

13.2 Mindful Activity 1: Listen to the Sounds

Ask the group to sit comfortably on a chair or the carpet and close their eyes and then focus on the sounds that they can hear.

Encourage them to use mindful listening, which means really paying attention to this one process and not being in any way distracted by their thoughts … simply 'letting them go'.

Talk about the sounds that you might hear that most people would not notice if they were not using 'mindful listening', for example, cars driving by outside, children playing outside, computers whirring, lights buzzing, clocks ticking, bees humming.

Ask everyone to pay attention to each sound and to then reflect on how it feels to listen in this way.

How is this different from 'normal' listening?

13.3 Mindful Activity 2: Mindful Music

Choose a piece of music to play to the group – preferably one which most of them will like.

Explain to the group that they should not think about the music, instead they should simply listen.

Encourage everyone to breathe deeply and slowly and to absorb the experience.

13.4 Mindful Activity 3: My Peaceful Place

Read the following script to the group and encourage everyone to try to return to their 'peaceful place' whenever they feel upset or stressed.

I would like to share one of my favourite places with you. I call it my Peaceful Place. It's not a place you travel to in a car, or a train, or a plane. It's a place inside you that you can visit just by closing your eyes. I am going to try to help you to find that place with me.

Close your eyes and take slow and deep breaths. Do this for at least three minutes. See if you can feel a kind of warm, happy smile in your body. Do you feel it? This is your Peaceful Place. Take some more deep breaths and really begin to feel very at home and comfortable in this special place.

The best thing about your Peaceful Place is that it's always inside you. You can visit it whenever you like. It is good to visit your Peaceful Place and feel the stillness that is there. It is helpful to visit your Peaceful Place if you are angry, lonely, sad or afraid. The Peaceful Place is a good place to talk with those feelings and to make friends with them. When you rest in your Peaceful Place and talk to your feelings, you may find that your feelings are not as big and as powerful as they seem. Remember, you can come here whenever you want and stay as long as you like.

(Saltzman & Goldin, 2008, p. 142.)

Bouncing Back & Coping With Change © Tina Rae 2016

13.5a Mindful Homework Tasks

You can use these mindfulness activities, as well as the ones we have done as a group, when you get home. Use the Mindfulness Activity Record to chart the activities you have tried, when you tried them, how they felt and what thoughts you had. You could give each activity a score out of 10.

Mindful Breaths

Being mindful means being aware of or noticing the present moment. Awareness helps us make choices about the present moment instead of acting like programmed robots.

Practise by sitting up straight and imagining you have a piece of string pulling the top of your head to the ceiling.

You can close your eyes if you want to. Think of this as your mindful sitting position. Imagine you hear the ring of a bell – this means you are ready to begin being mindful.

Practice bringing your attention into your breathing. You could do this by thinking in your head 'I am breathing in'.

While you breathe out, think to yourself 'I am breathing out'.

Notice the gap between your breath in and your breath out, and think, 'I am pausing between my breaths'.

If thoughts come into your head that is OK, just gently refocus on your breath and practise again breathing in, breathing out and noticing the pause between breaths.

The Raisin Task

Sit up straight in your mindful sitting position. Hold a raisin, or other small piece of food, carefully in your hand.

Look at it carefully, as if you are going to describe it to an alien who has never seen one before.

As best you can, be aware of thoughts or pictures that may come to your mind as you look at this raisin. Notice that they are just thoughts and then bring your attention back to this raisin.

Notice the colours of the raisin. Notice the surface of the raisin, whether it is bumpy or smooth.

Explore it by looking with your eyes and feeling with your fingers.
Notice whether it is dry or moist. Notice how the light shines on the raisin.

Bring the raisin to your nose. Notice if it has any smell.

Explore with your eyes, your fingers, and your nose.

Notice if your attention is on this raisin in your hand. Then, whenever you're ready, place the raisin in your mouth.

Explore the how the raisin feels in your mouth. Maybe you notice your mouth watering.

Keep your attention on the raisin and also notice your thoughts.

Maybe your thoughts are about looking forward to swallowing the raisin and eating another.

Maybe your thoughts are about noticing the sensations of the one that is in your mouth.

Gently bite the raisin. Taste the flavour. Slowly chew the raisin while noticing every sensation.

As you swallow the raisin, notice the intention to swallow it, then feel it slide down your throat and into your tummy.

Maybe you can feel that your body is now exactly one raisin heavier than it was a few minutes ago.

(Adapted from Semple & Lee 2008, pp.78–9.)

13.5b Mindfulness Activity Record

Date	Where	Activity	Sensations/Thoughts / Feelings	Score out of 10

Session 14
Relax Yourself

Introduction & Aims

To start, reinforce the group rules as agreed in Session 1, and then outline the key aims for the session and briefly summarise the proposed activities.

The aims of this session are:

- To understand and be able to recognise the qualities of a relaxed person.

- To introduce a relaxation script and for group members to make use of this.

- To make use of a visualisation technique to relax.

- For the group to reflect upon and identify their own skills in terms of managing to relax and wind down on a daily basis.

- For the group to make use of a diary format which provides them with an opportunity to plan their relaxation times for the coming week.

Icebreaker - A Question to Thought-Storm

Ask the question: 'What are the qualities or characteristics of a relaxed person?'
Ask everyone to contribute their own ideas and definitions. These can be written on a whiteboard or flipchart and it may then be useful for the group, as a whole, to come up with their own agreed list of qualities and attributes.

Group members may also wish to focus upon some of their personal attributes and identify some of the times when they have tried relaxation activities and highlight the impact that such strategies may have had on their overall well-being.

Warm-Up Game

Shopping
Ask everyone to sit in a circle and explain that you are going to start a shopping list and each person must add to it and remember what has come before. Begin by saying: 'I went shopping and I bought [name an item, for example, some bread]'. The person next to you repeats the sentence, including your item and adding one of their own. For example, 'I went shopping and I bought some bread and a tin of baked beans'. The next person must then repeat both items and their own, 'I went shopping and I bought I bought some bread, a tin of baked beans and a ham sandwich'. And so on around the circle.

This activity is above all a test of memory and you can encourage the group to try to use visualisation strategies or other means to remember each of the items. They should also think about ways in which they could support each other, non-verbally, in order to remember items should someone become stuck or confused. Can the group complete a whole circle?

Activities

14.1 Relaxation Practice – Take 10 Minutes to Chill

This initial activity introduces the group to the process of relaxation. Worksheet 14.1 offers them a script to follow in order to engage in this process as follows: tense each of the major muscle groups in your body for about 5 to 10 seconds and then RELAX. Be aware that some parts of your body may be more tense than others so pay more attention to these! PRACTISE this technique!

The idea is for everyone to be encouraged to make use of this strategy on a regular basis in order to reduce stress and increase their overall well-being.

14.2 Visualise Your Peaceful Place

This is another relaxation strategy and you can use the brief script on worksheet 14.2 to help and encourage the group to engage in writing about or drawing their own peaceful place.

14.3 My Own Relaxation Strategies

In this activity there is an opportunity for people to reflect upon and identify their own skills in terms of managing to relax and wind down on a daily basis. Using worksheet 14.3, ask them to complete the thought-storm 'What makes me relax and feel calm?'

14.4 My Relaxation Diary

Worksheet 14.4 is a diary that provides group members with the opportunity to plan their relaxation times for the coming week. Explain that they can use this diary to plan as many relaxation opportunities as possible over the next week. They should think of times when it might be helpful to stop, be still and feel calm. They could use some of the mindfulness techniques they have learned or perhaps a relaxation script, or listen to peaceful music or envisage their peaceful place. They should record what they did and when on the diary sheet and try to get into the relaxation habit to help keep themselves well both mentally and physically.

Feedback 4 Reflections

Ask the group to reflect upon what they have learnt in the session, posing the following questions:

- What was useful for you in this session?
- What might have made the session more useful for you?
- What have you learnt about yourself in today's session?
- What have you learnt about others?
- How will you use your knowledge and skills to help yourself and others in the future?

A Mindful Moment - The Feeling Recognition Game

Ask everyone to form a circle, either seated or standing, relaxed with feet apart.

1. Ask everyone to close their eyes and put their hands behind their backs while you place some small objects (for example, an eraser, a clothes-peg, small soft toy, a dice) in their hands.

2. Next, keeping eyes closed and the object behind their back, ask each person in turn to describe how their object feels, what they think it looks like, whether it is hard or soft, if they think it has a smell and what its shape is.

3. After each person has described their object, see if anyone else can guess what it is, and then ask the person to show their object to the group.

14.1 Relaxation Practice - Take 10 Minutes to Chill

This is a relaxation technique that you can practise and use to help you to relax if you are feeling stressed or you need to calm down.

To begin with, try to tense each of the major muscle groups in your body for about 5 to 10 seconds and then **relax**. Remember what this feels like. Be aware that some parts of your body may be more tense than others so pay more attention to these!

Now practise this technique!

Step 1: Choose a quiet, warm and comfortable place.

Step 2: Sit in a comfortable chair or lie on your bed.

Step 3: Make sure you won't be disturbed.

Step 4: First tense and then relax your muscles in your:

(a) right foot

(b) entire right leg

(c) left foot

(d) entire left leg

(e) right hand

(f) entire right arm

(g) left hand

(h) entire left arm

(i) abdomen

(j) chest

(k) neck and shoulders

(l) face

Step 5: REPEAT

Step 6: Close your eyes and count slowly to 100

14.2 Visualise Your Peaceful Place

Close your eyes and visualise your most peaceful place – what does it look, feel, smell and sound like?

Create and hold this image in your mind and then use words or pictures to describe in the space below:

14.3 My Own Relaxation Strategies

Thought-Storm! What makes you relax and feel calm?

List your ideas below.

What helps me to relax and feel calm?

_____

_____

_____

_____

Now think about how you would create your own relaxation plan. Identify your three most stressful situations and the strategies you could now use to try to keep calmer and stay more relaxed in each situation. Try them out!

My three stressful situations:

1. _____

2. _____

3. _____

My new strategies for feeling calm:

_____

_____

_____

14.4 My Relaxation Diary

Use this diary to plan as many relaxation opportunities as possible over the next week – think of times when you might have to stop, be still and feel calm. You could use some of the mindfulness techniques, a relaxation script, listen to peaceful music or envisage your peaceful place. Record what you did and when on the chart below. Try to get into the relaxation habit so you keep yourself well both mentally and physically.

	Monday	Tuesday	Wednesday	Thursday	Friday	Saturday	Sunday
9.00am							
11.00am							
1.00pm							
3.00pm							
5.00pm							
7.00pm							
9.00pm							
11.00pm							

Feeling Friendly

Introduction & Aims

To begin with, reinforce the group rules as agreed in Session 1, and then outline the key aims for the session and briefly summarise the proposed activities.

The aims of this session are:

- To recognise the qualities and attributes of a friendly person.

- To give and receive positive thoughts and feel good about themselves and others.

- To identify people's own circles of friendship.

- To engage in a self-reflection activity in which the group are specifically asked to reflect upon their own skills of friendship and identify and rate their own skills.

- To make use of a strategy to boost the self-esteem and confidence of their friend by focusing upon all their strengths and positive qualities.

Icebreaker - A Question to Thought-Storm

Ask the question: 'What are the qualities of a friendly person?'
Ask everyone to contribute their own ideas and definitions. These can be written on a whiteboard or flipchart and it may then be useful for the group, as a whole, to come up with their own agreed list of qualities and attributes.

The group may also wish to focus upon some of their own attributes and identify some of the times when they have been a good friend or shown kindness to others and the impact of these behaviours.

Warm-Up Game

Positive Points
This is an opportunity for everyone in the group to both give and receive positive thoughts and to feel good about themselves and others. You will need to prepare a list of positive statements beforehand. These can be photocopied onto cards so that the group members can quickly cut them out. Ideally, come up with a list of about ten positive statements. These could include:

- You are always kind.
- You look very smart.
- You have a nice smile.
- You work hard.
- You're friendly and thoughtful.
- You're kind to others.
- You have neat writing.
- You are good at sports.

Give a list to each person in the group and ask them to cut out the statements. Now divide the group into smaller groups of two or three. Ask each person to choose a positive statement from their list to give to each member of their group. When everyone has received their statements, the group can return to the circle. Discuss how it felt to receive these positive comments, ensuring that everyone gives some feedback.

Activities

15.1 Feeling Friendly – A Thought-Storm

This activity gives the group the opportunity to reflect upon the qualities and attributes of a good friend. Worksheet 15.1 uses a thought-storm format to pose the following questions: What is a 'good' friend? What are their skills and qualities?

Ask the group members to work on their own at first, and then compare their answers with others. Do people have similar definitions of friendship? Why are friends so important for our well-being and happiness?

15.2 Friendship Circles

Using worksheet 15.2, ask the group to think about and identify their own circles of friendship. Ask them to complete the Friendship Circles by writing the names of their best friends in Circle 1; write the names of next-best friends in Circle 2; write the names of hardly-friends-at-all in Circle 3. Now ask everyone to write the qualities they think belong to the people in each of the three circles provided.

Now think about and discuss whether people think they share any or all of these qualities? Finally, think about how your friends in Circle 1 would describe you.

15.3 Focus on my Friendship Skills

This is a self-reflection activity in which the group are specifically asked to reflect upon their own skills of friendship. Ask everyone to identify and rate their own skills using the following instructions:

- Stop, think and reflect.
- How are your friendship skills? What kind of friend are you? How are your skills?

- Rate yourself against each statement in the list. Rate yourself honestly on the scale.

- Use 1 for 'Not a lot', 3 for 'OK', 5 for 'Always'

Ask the group to think carefully and to identify areas that they may need to develop and improve on in the future.

15.4   A Friendly Message in a Bottle

For this final activity, ask everyone to come up with a special message which they would place in a bottle and send to someone who means a lot to them and who has shown them genuine friendship.

The idea of this activity is to boost the self-esteem and confidence of their friend by focusing on all their strengths and positive qualities.

Feedback 4 Reflections

Ask the group to reflect upon what they have learnt in the session, posing the following questions:

- What was useful for you in this session?

- What might have made the session more useful for you?

- What have you learnt about yourself in today's session?

- What have you learnt about others?

- How will you use your knowledge and skills to help yourself and others in the future?

A Mindful Moment – Mindful Drawing

Select an object to be drawn, such as a vase containing flowers or a fruit bowl containing a selection of fruit. Ask the group to draw the chosen item, reinforcing the importance of really looking, observing and concentrating on what it looks like. However, they will only be allowed to look at the object for 30 seconds, after which you will cover it with a cloth as they will not be allowed look at it while they draw.

When everyone has finished their drawing, ask them to compare their pictures with the actual object. Which parts are closest to reality and which aren't quite right? Reinforce that this isn't a competition, more of an experiment to see what happens.

If people want to, and there is adequate time, they can repeat the exercise and see how much better the second drawing is through paying closer attention.
Repeat the comparison – have the drawings improved?

15.1 Feeling Friendly - A Thought-Storm

What is a 'good' friend? What are their skills and qualities?

Use the thought bubbles below for your answers and ideas.

Work on your own at first, and then compare your answers with others in the group.

Do we share similar definitions of friendship?

Why are friends so important for our well-being and happiness?

15.2 Friendship Circles

Complete the Friendship Circles below:

- Write the names of your best friends in Circle 1
- Write the names of your next-best friends in Circle 2
- Write the names of hardly-friends-at-all in Circle 3

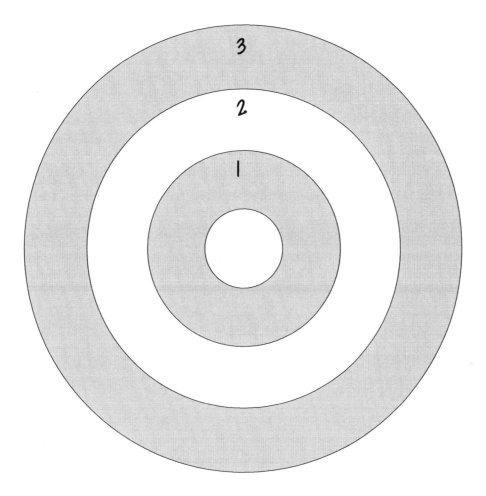

Write the qualities you think belong to the people in each of the three circles:

Circle 1 qualities include: _____

Circle 2 qualities include: _____

Circle 3 qualities include: _____

Do you share any or all of these qualities?

_____

How would your friends in Circle 1 describe you?

15.3 Focus on My Friendship Skills

Stop, think and reflect.

How are your friendship skills? What kind of friend are you?

Rate yourself against each statement in the list. Make sure you are as honest as possible.
Scale: 1 = 'Not a lot', 3 = 'OK', 5 = 'Always'

Statement	My rating				
1. I can listen properly to my friends.	1	2	3	4	5
2. I don't judge them.	1	2	3	4	5
3. I respect their views and feelings.	1	2	3	4	5
4. I am honest with my friends about my views and feelings.	1	2	3	4	5
5. I can tell my friends that I don't agree with them.	1	2	3	4	5
6. I don't talk about friends behind their backs.	1	2	3	4	5
7. I don't put my friends down.	1	2	3	4	5
8. I try not to take my problems out on my friends.	1	2	3	4	5
9. I can recognise and empathise with how my friends are feeling.	1	2	3	4	5
10. I can motivate my friends to do their best.	1	2	3	4	5
11. I can support them with they feel down.	1	2	3	4	5
12. I don't try to push my friends into doing what I want to do.	1	2	3	4	5
13. I can respect that they are different to me in some ways.	1	2	3	4	5
14. I can cope with the fact that they might need to be on their own sometimes.	1	2	3	4	5
15. I can cope with the fact that they have other friends.	1	2	3	4	5

Stop and think!

Can you be a better friend?

Where are your strongest skills?

Where do you need to improve your skills?

15.4 A Friendly Message in a Bottle

Write a note to a friend to help to build their self-esteem and confidence. Tell them about all the things that they have done well and how they have helped and supported you and their other friends.

Tell your friend about how you feel about having them as a friend and how you would like to support them in the future.

Send the message to your friend!

Session 16

Boosting Positive Emotions

Introduction & Aims

To start, reinforce the group rules as agreed in Session 1, and then outline the key aims for the session and briefly summarise the proposed activities.

The aims of this session are:

- To understand what we can do in order to be able to boost positive emotions – both in ourselves and others.

- To reinforce the fact that we are in control of ourselves and that emotions do not control us.

- To reinforce the importance of accepting ourselves and others.

- To understand how remembering positive events and people can boost our positive feelings and overall sense of well-being.

- To create 'compliments cards' for people who are special to group members and who have made a difference to them in their lives, in order to show gratitude and boost their positive emotions.

Icebreaker - A Question to Thought-Storm

Ask the question: 'What can we do to boost positive feelings?'
Ask everyone to contribute their own ideas and definitions. These can be written on a whiteboard or flipchart and it may then be useful for the group, as a whole, to come up with their own agreed list of ideas. Group members may also wish to focus upon some of their own attributes and to identify some of the times when they have tried to increase their own positive feelings. Discuss what worked best, thinking about any similarities in people's strategies.

Warm-Up Game

Copy the Clap
This is an action-copying game which can be played at great speed. Ask everyone to form a circle and then start the game by performing a simple action. For example, crouch down and touch the floor or jump up and down. Everyone must then clap twice, and then you should name and point to a person in the circle. They must copy the action and then think of

one of their own to show to the group. Everyone claps twice again and the performer names and points to another person, who in turn copies the last action and then acts their own. This activity continues until everyone has taken a turn to copy and follow the actions around the circle.

The aim is to have no disruption or hesitation in the flow of the game so everyone must focus and remain alert and be ready to respond as they never know when it will be their turn.

Activities

16.1   Boosting Positive Emotions – ACT!

In this activity, the group is introduced to ways of boosting their own positive emotions and managing to be in control of these in order to maintain well-being. It is vital to reinforce the fact that we can be in control of ourselves and that emotions do not control us. Give everyone a copy of worksheet 16.1 and emphasise that there are many different ways of managing emotions and boosting well-being. These can be placed under three headings:

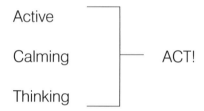

Divide into smaller groups and thought-storm and identify as many different interventions as possible under each of the three headings provided. An example of each is provided on worksheet 16.1 to prompt thinking and discussion.

16.2   Boosting Positive Emotions Acceptance Cards – It's Good to be You!

This is an activity that can be played in small groups of 6 to 8. Give each group a copy of worksheet 16.2 and ask them to cut out the cards in order to play the Acceptance Game. Each group should nominate one person to shuffle the cards and then begin by taking the top card, completing the sentence or answering the question. The card is returned to the bottom of the pile and the next person takes a card, continuing around the group. If someone can't think of an answer, they can then take another card or pass if they are really stuck.

16.3   Positively Remembering

Discuss in the group how remembering past events, situations or people with love and affection and in a positive way can be a very important way of maintaining well-being. It can be particularly useful to develop the ability to transport yourself to positive past times when times get tough or challenging.

Ask the group members to create their Positive Memories Collage on worksheet 16.3 and include events, people and objects that continue to make them feel good about themselves and positive about their lives in general.

16.4   Boosting the Positive Emotions of Others – Create Your Compliments Cards

For this final activity ask group members to think about boosting positive emotions in others, by creating their own compliments cards for the people who are special to them and who have made a difference to them in their lives. They can have as many copies of worksheet 16.4 as they need.

Feedback & Reflections

Ask the group to reflect upon what they have learnt in the session, posing the following questions:

- What was useful for you in this session?
- What might have made the session more useful for you?
- What have you learnt about yourself in today's session?
- What have you learnt about others?
- How will you use your knowledge and skills to help yourself and others in the future?

A Mindful Moment – Listen to the Bell!

Ask the group to sit on their chairs or the floor with their hands on their stomachs. Now ask them to feel their breathing – breathe in and out with their hands on their stomachs and listen carefully to their breath and feel how it moves their bodies.

Once everyone has settled, ring a bell several times. Ask everyone to think about how many times they hear the bell.

Stress that there is no right or wrong answer – the question is just 'How many times did you hear the bell?'

Repeat the activity.

Ask the group to reflect on the following questions:

- Why do you think you may not have heard the bell every time?
- Did your mind wander?
- Where did your attention go?
- Where is it now?'

16.1 Boosting Positive Emotions - ACT!

A key point to remember: YOU are in control and NOT your emotions!

There are many different ways of managing emotions and boosting well-being. These can be placed under 3 headings:

Active

Calming — ACT!

Thinking

In your small group thought-storm and identify as many different interventions as you can under each of the three headings. An example of each has been provided.

Active Techniques	Calming Techniques	Thinking Techniques
Dancing	Relaxation scripts	Reframing

16.2 Boosting Positive Emotions Acceptance Cards - It's Good to be You!

Cut out the cards and play the Acceptance Game!

In your group choose one person to shuffle the cards and then start by taking the top card, and completing the sentence or answering the question. Return the card to the bottom of the pile and then continue around the group until all the cards have been used.

If you are really stuck, you can take another card or pass on your turn.

I'm good at ...	Say two things you like about the person opposite.	I know I'm successful when ...
I'm getting better at ...	I know when others accept me because ...	My best point is ...
My main strengths are ...	My mum or dad or carer thinks I'm good at ...	My best day was ...
I think my friends like me because ...	I know that my mum or dad or carer accepts me for who I am because ...	My friends like me because ...
I like myself because ...	I feel positive when ...	My best subject is ...
I care a lot about ...	If you could be anyone else in the group who would it be and why?	The best bit about how I look is ...
What is most important to me is ...	It's Good to be You!	My greatest talent is ...
I feel important when ...	Tell the person opposite what people like about him or her.	I know I have the power to ...
My best achievement is ...	In this game I most respect [person's name] because ...	My best quality is ...
Turn to the person on your right and identify two positive things about them.	I feel confident when ...	Turn to the person on your left and identify two positive things about them.

16.3 Positively Remembering

Remembering past events, situations or people with love and affection and in a positive way is a very important way of maintaining well-being. It is particularly useful to develop the ability to transport yourself to positive past times when things get tough or challenging.

Using words or pictures, create your Positive Memories Collage and include events, people and objects that continue to make you feel good about yourself and positive about your life!

My Positive Memories Collage

16.4 Boosting the Positive Emotions of Others - Create Your Compliments Cards

Send a private compliment using the notecard; you can make as many cards as you need.

FOLD

FOLD & SEAL

The Savouring Habit

Introduction & Aims

To start, reinforce the group rules as agreed in Session 1, and then outline the key aims for the session and briefly summarise the proposed activities.

The aims of this session are:

- To understand the concept and process of savouring.

- To consider how the ability to savour the moment might increase people's levels of happiness.

- To think about and record the things that people have savoured in the past, things they can savour now and things that they can savour in the future.

- To understand the importance of being able to stop and savour the good things that happen.

- For group members to keep a savouring scroll and recognise the need to engage in this process on a daily basis.

Icebreaker - A Question to Thought-Storm

Ask the question: 'Why is it important to savour good times and positive experiences in our lives?'

Ask everyone to contribute their own ideas and definitions. These can be written on a whiteboard or flipchart and it may then be useful for the group, as a whole, to come up with their own agreed list of situations and experiences. The group may wish to focus on some of their personal experiences and consider how the ability to savour the moment might increase their levels of happiness overall.

Warm-Up Game

Clockwise or Anti-Clockwise

Ask everyone to form a circle. You are going to send two different actions around the circle simultaneously. For example, squeezing the hand of the person on your left to move around the circle in a clockwise direction, and a tap on the elbow of the person on your right to travel in an anti-clockwise direction. The idea is for both of actions to arrive back with you simultaneously. Group members need to be alert to not passing on an action before they've actually received it. It will also be helpful if they watch carefully as to how the actions are travelling around the circle in order to synchronise their speeds. You can then chose individuals to pass around movements themselves for additional rounds.

Session 17 The Savouring Habit

Activities

17.1   Savouring Situations

Ask the group to focus on the concept of savouring and discuss the definitions provided on worksheet 17.1. Bryant & Veroff (2006) define savouring as any thoughts or behaviours capable of 'generating, intensifying and prolonging enjoyment'.

Martin Seligman (2003) says that the ability to savour the positive experiences we have is one of the most important elements of happiness. Savouring situations fosters positive emotions and increases our overall well-being.

Working individually and then in the whole group ask everyone to consider answers to the questions on the worksheet which will help people to reflect upon their own savouring behaviours and skills.

17.2   Savouring in the Past, the Now and the Future!

For this activity ask the members of the group to think about and record on worksheet 17.2 the things that they have savoured in the past, things they can savour now and things that they can savour in the future.

17.3   My Savouring Scroll

Sometimes we forget to stop and savour the good things that happen to us. Ask the group to keep a savouring scroll on worksheet 17.3 using these instructions:

> Every evening, think of one thing (at least) that has happened during the day when you were able to stop, think and reflect and *savour* the moment or experience. Record these times on your scroll. At the end of the week *look* at the list – now you'll know that positive things really do happen to you and that you can, and do, savour them!

Feedback & Reflections

Ask the group to reflect upon what they have learnt in the session, posing the following questions:

- What was useful for you in this session?
- What might have made the session more useful for you?
- What have you learnt about yourself in today's session?
- What have you learnt about others?
- How will you use your knowledge and skills to help yourself and others in the future?

A Mindful Moment - Five Things Activity

Introduce this activity with the following script:

> In this exercise, all you need to do is notice five things in your day that usually go unnoticed. They could be things you hear, smell, feel on your body, or see. For example, you might see the street surface, hear the birds sing, feel your clothes or smell the flowers or freshly cut grass. Of course you may already do these things, but are you really aware of them and what they mean for you? What resonance do they have for you?

17.1 Savouring Situations

What is savouring?

Bryant & Veroff (2006) define savouring as any thoughts or behaviours capable of 'generating, intensifying and prolonging enjoyment'.

Martin Seligman (2003) says that the ability to savour the positive experiences we have is one of the most important elements of happiness. Savouring situations fosters positive emotions and increases our overall well-being.

Questions to Consider

1. What are your most enjoyable activities?

2. How frequently do you **stop** and **savour** these experiences?

3. How do you savour these activities?

4. When do you savour these activities?

5. What prevents you from savouring?

6. Why do we sometimes just 'rush through' an activity such as eating?

7. Why do we not take the time to simply stop and take in our surroundings?

8. Why do you think we have to make 'savouring' a deliberate act?

17.2 Savouring in the Past, the Now and the Future!

Think about the things that you have savoured in the past, things you can savour now and things that you can savour in the future.

Record these on the chart below and then SAVOUR!

Things I can savour from the PAST	Things I can savour NOW	Things I can savour in the FUTURE
Think about holidays, time spent with friends/family, early childhood.	Think about friends, food, books, movies, hobbies.	Think about a career or job, relationships, friends, holidays, exam or work success.

17.3 My Savouring Scroll

Sometimes we forget to stop and savour the good things that happen – this is **not good**!

Every evening, think of one thing (at least!) that has happened during the day when you were able to stop, think and reflect and **savour** the moment or experience. Record these times on your scroll. At the end of the week **look** at your list – now you'll know that positive things really do happen to you and that you can, and do, savour them!

Session 18
Showing the Gratitude

Introduction & Aims

To start, reinforce the group rules as agreed in Session 1, and then outline the key aims for the session and briefly summarise the proposed activities.

The aims of this session are:

- To identify the qualities of a grateful person.
- To understand and appreciate the importance of showing gratitude.
- To understand that being grateful is about much more than just saying thank you – it's about not taking things for granted and having a sense of appreciating the good things that happen to us in our lives.
- To be aware that people who are grateful tend to be happier, healthier and more fulfilled.
- Awareness that being grateful can help people cope with stress and can even have a beneficial effect on heart rate.
- To devise a letter of thanks to show gratitude to a special person in people's lives and to appreciate the importance of engaging in such an activity.

Icebreaker - A Question to Thought-Storm

Ask the question: 'What are the qualities of a grateful person?'
Ask everyone to contribute their own ideas and definitions. These can be written on a whiteboard or flipchart and it may then be useful for the group, as a whole, to come up with their own agreed list of qualities and attributes. Group members may wish to focus on some of their own attributes and identify some of the times when they have shown gratitude towards others and the feelings that resulted.

Warm-Up Game

Disagree or Agree
Ask everyone to form a circle and then pair up with the person sitting directly next to them. Now walk around the circle labelling alternate pairs as either an 'agree pair' or a 'disagree pair'. Next, read out a series of statements, and explain to the pairs that they are to work in groups in order to come up with reasons why they would disagree or agree with each of the statements. These might include the following examples:

- Girls are better readers than boys.

- Money doesn't make you happy.

- Dogs make better pets than cats.

- Television is not good for young people.

- Happy people live longer than unhappy people.

- All children should wear school uniform.

- Girls should not be allowed to go out with boys until they are 17 years old.

- Women should always stay at home and look after their children.

- Bullies are sad people.

- Boys should not cry.

- Children should do less homework.

The 'agree' and 'disagree' groups can then feed back to the whole group their reasons for disagreeing or agreeing with each of the statements.

Activities

18.1 Thought-Storm – When am I Grateful?

The aim of this activity is for group members to identify those things for which they are grateful while at the same time focusing on their behaviour in relation to these things – what do they do and what don't they do in terms of showing their gratitude? Use worksheet 18.1 to record thoughts and then discuss in the whole group.

18.2 A Daily Event: Three Good Things – Be Grateful!

Discuss in the group how being grateful is about much more than just saying thank you. It is about not taking things for granted and having a sense of appreciating the good things that happen to us in our lives. People who are grateful tend to be happier, healthier and more fulfilled. Being grateful can help people cope with stress and can even have a beneficial effect on heart rate.

Ask the group to write down, over a one week period, three good things that happen to them each day. These can be anything that they feel good about or grateful for.

18.3 Write a Letter of Thanks – or Three!

Studies have shown that expressing gratitude to others can significantly boost our happiness. Ask everyone to think about and identify the people to whom they are really grateful. Give each person a copy of worksheet 18.3a and 18.3b.

Ask each person to think of three people who have been a really positive influence in their lives and who they feel really grateful to. These could be family members, an old teacher, a friend, or someone else who has made a real difference in their lives. Use worksheet 18.3a to help think about these people, what they did and how it affected people's lives.

Now each person should use worksheet 18.3b to write a letter of thanks to one (or more) of the people they have identified. The important thing here is that the gratitude should come from the heart and really inform the person concerned that they have been a force for good in someone's life.

Feedback & Reflections

Ask the group to reflect upon what they have learnt in the session, posing the following questions:

- What was useful for you in this session?
- What might have made the session more useful for you?
- What have you learnt about yourself in today's session?
- What have you learnt about others?
- How will you use your knowledge and skills to help yourself and others in the future?

A Mindful Moment – The Suitcase Activity

Ask everyone to imagine they have been given a suitcase in which to pack all the important things in their lives at the moment. They can spend some time being mindful of all the people, places, things and thoughts that they feel are the most important to them. They can then draw, write or add pictures of their choices around a picture of a suitcase or simply describe these to a partner, telling them why they have made these choices in such a mindful way.

Session 18 Showing the Gratitude

18.1 Thought-Storm - When am I Grateful?

What do I do?

What don't I do?

18.2 A Daily Event: Three Good Things - Be Grateful!

Being grateful is about much more than just saying thank you – it's about not taking things for granted and having a sense of appreciating the good things that happen to us in our lives.

People who are grateful tend to be happier, healthier and more fulfilled. Being grateful can help people cope with stress and can even have a beneficial effect on heart rate.

Each day, write down three good things that have happened to you. These can be anything that you feel good about or grateful for.

- To get used to the idea, start by filling in the boxes below to describe three good things that happened to you **yesterday** and why they were good.
- Try to include **why** you felt each of the things was really good.

Good Thing 1
Good Thing 2
Good Thing 3

Now repeat this activity **at the end of each day** for a week. How do you then feel at the end of the week? Think about this and discuss with a friend or family member. Did this make a difference to your overall sense of happiness and well-being?

18.3a Write A Letter of Thanks - or Three!

Studies show that expressing gratitude to others can significantly boost our happiness. Who are you really grateful to?

- Think of three people who have been a really positive influence in your life and that you feel really grateful to. They could be family members, an old teacher, a friend, or anyone else who has made a real difference in your life.

Person 1: Who is it and why are you grateful to them?
Person 2: Who is it and why are you grateful to them?
Person 3: Who is it and why are you grateful to them?

- Now choose one of these people to write to and tell them how grateful you are: perhaps you could choose someone you have not thanked properly before.

- Think about the impact this person had on you and what you would write in a letter to them. Consider the following:

  - What specifically you are grateful for;

  - How they helped you;

  - How they helped to make you the person you are today.

Use worksheet 18.3b to write the letter anyway you like – but really try to think about how it feels to be grateful to them as you write.
You may then also want to write to the other two people!

Stop & Reflect

Who did you write your letter of gratitude to? How did it feel?

18.3b My Letter of Thanks

Dear...

Session 19
The Growth Mindset

Introduction & Aims

To start, reinforce the group rules as agreed in Session 1, and then outline the key aims for the session and briefly summarise the proposed activities.

The aims of this session are:

- To understand the qualities of an open-minded person.
- To support the group in beginning to consider how to develop and maintain a growth mindset and how can they do this in practical terms.
- To present and make use of a structured process for managing and meeting a challenge.

Icebreaker - A Question to Thought-Storm

Ask the question: 'What are the qualities of an open-minded person?'

Ask everyone to contribute their own ideas and definitions. These can be written on a whiteboard or flipchart and it may then be useful for the group, as a whole, to come up with their own agreed list of qualities and attributes. They may also wish to focus upon some of their own attributes and identify some of the times when they have been open-minded and prepared to take risks and face up to challenges with a positive outlook.

Warm-Up Game

Feeling Lines Activity

Give each group member plain pieces of A4 paper and make available a selection of coloured pencils or pens. Now give each person the name of a feeling which they are then asked to commit to memory. These might include the following: happy, sad, angry, upset, nervous, unconfident, contented, lonely. Ensure that each feeling is given to more than one person. Now ask everyone to draw a line on their sheet of paper to represent the feeling that they have been given. This can be done to a time limit, for example, 2 minutes. The line must start on one side of the paper and finish on the other but it can be any colour, thickness or shape. When everyone has finished, ask people to group themselves according to the feeling that they have been given and compare their lines, discussing why they drew the line as they did. One person from each group may wish to act as the scribe so that each group can feedback on what they have committed to paper. Alternatively, the whole group may wish to go round the circle and describe what they have drawn and why they have drawn the feeling in this particular way.

Activities

19.1   Is Your Mindset Fixed?

Using worksheet 19.1, ask everyone to make a list of things they feel they are good at and things they feel they are bad at. Then ask them to consider the following questions:

- Do you think you can get even better at the things you are good at?
- Do you think you will always be good at the things you are good at now?
- What would happen if you failed at any of these good skills or activities?
- Have you always been bad at the things you have listed on your 'Bad' list?
- Do you think you can get better at any of the things on your 'Bad' list?
- What might be preventing you from doing this?
- What might help you to get better at these things?

The idea is to support the group in beginning to consider how to develop and maintain a growth mindset – how can they do this? What are the right questions to ask?

19.2   Change Your Behaviour – Change Your Life! Get a Growth Mindset!

In this thought-storm activity, ask everyone to identify the following:

- Things I would like to do more often.
- Things I would like to do better.
- Times I would like to be happier.

Now ask everyone to write or draw their ideas on worksheet 19.2.

19.3   Take Up The Challenge

Worksheet 19.3 outlines a structured process for managing and meeting a challenge. Look through the different steps together as a group and think about possible answers or strategies for each stage. Now each person can think about their personal challenge and try to fill in the steps on their worksheet.

Once people get used to breaking down a challenge into these steps, they can generalise it across a range of different contexts in the future.

Session 19 The Growth Mindset

Feedback & Reflections

Ask the group to reflect upon what they have learnt in the session, posing the following questions:

- What was useful for you in this session?
- What might have made the session more useful for you?
- What have you learnt about yourself in today's session?
- What have you learnt about others?
- How will you use your knowledge and skills to help yourself and others in the future?

A Mindful Moment – Pass the Drawing Activity

Give each person a piece of paper and ask them to write their initials on the reverse.

Now ask them to think of something that they'd like to draw and to begin drawing it.

After 40 seconds, tell everyone to stop and swap their piece of paper with the person to their left, and without talking to each other, to continue the other's drawing. After another minute tell everyone to put down their pens.

They can then discuss the end result.

How did they feel about doing this?

What could they do to be really good at this exercise?

19.1 Is Your Mindset Fixed?

Make a list of things you feel you are **good** at doing and things you feel you are **bad** at doing. Then consider the questions below.

Things I am good at...	Things I am bad at...

- Do you think you can get even better at the things you are good at?
- Do you think you will always be good at the things you are good at now?
- What would happen if you failed at any of these good skills or activities?
- Have you always been bad at the things you have listed on your bad list?
- Do you think you can get better at any of the things on your bad list?
- What might be preventing you?
- What might help you to get better at these things?

19.2 Change Your Behaviour - Change Your Life! Get a Growth Mindset!

Thought-storm about the following:

- Things I would like to do more often.
- Things I would like to do better.
- Times I would like to be happier.

Write or draw them below.

19.3 Take Up The Challenge

My Main Challenge is:
Stage 1: My Steps to Succeed are:
Stage 2: My Coping self-talk is:
Stage 3: Visualise Yourself being Successful!   Repeat your coping self-talk while you imagine reaching your 1st step! Keep practising this.
Stage 4: Experiment!   Pick a time to face your fear or challenge - try it out - take your first step and use your self-talk.
Stage 5: Reward!   Treat yourself for being successful!

Don't give up! Keep going!

Break the steps down into smaller ones if you don't succeed at first!

Session 20

Focus on Future Solutions

Introduction & Aims

To start, reinforce the group rules as agreed in Session 1, and then outline the key aims for the session and briefly summarise the proposed activities.

The aims of this session are:

- To identify the qualities of a good problem-solver.
- To think of three things they could do or change about themselves now in order to become their 'best' person.
- To identify the strengths that they could use in the process of meeting such a goal.
- To each identify one bad habit to dump and to be able to identify the small steps that will need to taken along the way to doing this.
- To identify the things people are going to do to make their dreams and ambitions for the future come true.
- To identify personal goals for the future and for each person to identify their priority goal which they can begin to work towards now.

Icebreaker - A Question to Thought-Storm

Ask the question: 'What are the qualities of a good problem-solver?'
Ask everyone to contribute their own ideas and definitions. These can be written on a whiteboard or flipchart and it may then be useful for the group, as a whole, to come up with their own agreed list of qualities and attributes. The group may also wish to focus upon some of their own attributes and identify some of the times when they have engaged in effective problem-solving, discussing the strategies they used and how they managed to keep focused on identifying a solution.

Warm-Up Game

Tangled Web
This activity requires a ball of wool and involves everyone sitting in a circle. Give one person the ball of wool and ask them to throw it to someone they have a connection with, making sure they hold on to the end of the wool and at the same time saying what that connection is. The connection can be anything – for example, having the same colour hair, living in the same road, going to the same club. The recipient grabs hold of the wool so that it forms a

link between themselves and the person who has thrown it. They then throw the ball of wool to someone else, identifying a new or different connection, and again making sure they hold on to the wool. This is repeated until everyone has had a turn and there is a web of wool across the circle.

This is a very visual and striking demonstration of the ways in which we are all linked and connected to one another. It highlights similarities and differences and is a good reminder of the need to value diversity.

Activities

20.1 My Best Future Person
This is a version of the ideal-self activity which emanates from Personal Construct Psychology (PCP) (Kelly, 1955). Ask the group the following question:
If you had a magic wand and could change yourself, what would you change?

Give each person a copy of worksheet 20.1 and ask them to draw and write their ideas for change in the spaces provided. Once they have done this, everyone should take some time to Stop, Think and Reflect.

Now ask them to think of three things they could do or change about themselves in order to become their 'best' person. What strengths could they use in this process? Which of the tools they have learnt in these sessions would help the most? Form pairs and share thoughts with a partner.

20.2 Focus on Solutions – Bin that Bad Habit!
In this activity, group members are encouraged to bin their bad habits. Give everyone worksheet 20.2 and a blank sheet of paper.

First, ask them to write down on the blank sheet all of their 'bad' habits and put them in order – those that are easiest to stop at the bottom and those that are hardest to stop at the top.

Now ask everyone to identify one bad habit to dump. Think about how to do this, identifying small steps on the way. Use worksheet 20.2 to set out strategies and ideas.

20.3 Self-Reflection Activity – The Best Possible Future
Explain to the group that in this is a self-reflection activity in which they will need to focus on their futures and be very honest about their ambitions and dreams. Worksheet 20.3 asks them to identify the things they are going to do to make their dreams and ambitions for the future come true. They must then think about which skills they can use to help them do so.

20.4 Setting My Goals
Give everyone a copy of worksheet 20.4. Encourage people to think about and write down, under the different headings, their goals for the future. Now each person should think about one goal which could become their priority and that they can begin to work on now. The

worksheet shows a clear process that can be followed to check whether this goal is a good one to choose. It includes the following steps:

Think about your Priority Goal and ask yourself two questions:
1. On a scale of 1 to 10 how much good will come if I achieve this goal and everything turns out well?
2. On a scale of 1 to 10 how much will my life be affected if I don't achieve this goal or things do not turn out well?

Think about your answers:
- If your answer to 1 is higher than your answer to 2, it is clear you should go for it.
- If your answer to 2 is higher than your answer to 1, think about a different goal.
- If your answers to 1 and 2 are the same, think about how you can increase the upside. Then just do it!
- If you can't think of an upside, don't do anything and think about your goal again tomorrow.

The process provides the group with a strategy for goal-setting that they can use across a range of situations.

It might be helpful to allow some additional time at the end of the session to enable the group to share their aspirations and to encourage each other to meet these goals and build on their capacity to engage in happy habits that promote and maintain their well-being.

Feedback & Reflections

Ask the group to reflect upon what they have learnt in the session, posing the following questions:
- What was useful for you in this session?
- What might have made the session more useful for you?
- What have you learnt about yourself in today's session?
- What have you learnt about others?
- How will you use your knowledge and skills to help yourself and others in the future?

A Mindful Moment – The WOW! Factor

Ask the group following question: What are the things that fill you with wonder? Think about what these could be: a rainbow, how you breathe, a new baby, a mountain, the sea, a butterfly, a bluebell wood or a whale.

The next steps can be done either as individuals or as a group project.

Materials:

- Paper or thin card for each person
- Thick and thin felt tips

Explain the method to the group as follows:

- Create a big cartoon-style 'WOW!' in the middle of your sheet of paper.

- Use bright colours to make your 'WOW!' and draw zigzag shapes around it with a thick felt tip so it looks like a word from a cartoon.

- Think about all the things that fill you with wonder and make you want to say 'WOW!' and all the things that give you a special tingly feeling when you think about them.

- Your 'WOW!'s could be things in nature, being loved in a special way, doing something amazing, a new baby or being in a beautiful place. Maybe they are rainbows or crashing waves, or bees or being on a mountain. Maybe they are being close to a waterfall, being hugged, a special piece of music, a tree or being in a place of worship.

- Write or draw your 'WOW!'s or moments of wonder all around your 'WOW!' word.

- Tell each other about your favourite 'WOW!' MOMENTS.

20.1 My Best Future Person

If you had a magic wand and could change yourself, what things would you change?

Draw and label them below.

Stop, think and reflect.

Think of three things you could do or change about yourself now in order to become your 'best' person.

What strengths could you use in this process?

Which of the tools that you have learned would help you most?

Share your thoughts with a partner.

20.2 Focus on Solutions - Bin that Bad Habit!

First, on a separate sheet, write down all your 'bad' habits and put them in order with the ones that are easiest to stop at the bottom and the ones that are hardest at the top.

Now, choose one of your bad habits to dump.

THE HABIT I WANT TO DUMP IS:

Write down the small steps you can take to achieve success.

MY STEPS TO SUCCESS

1

2

3

4

5

How will you keep calm? What is your coping self-talk?

HOW I WILL KEEP CALM

MY SELF-TALK

Who else can help or support you and how?

PEOPLE WHO CAN HELP ME

1

2

3

HOW THEY CAN HELP

1

2

3

Go for it! Reward yourself and don't give up!

20.3 Self-Reflection Activity - The Best Possible Future

These are the things I am going to do to make my dreams and ambitions for the future come true:

1 _____

2 _____

3 _____

4 _____

These are the strengths I can draw on and the skills I can use in order to help me to make my dreams and ambitions for the future come true:

1 _____

2 _____

3 _____

4 _____

20.4 Setting My Goals

My Friendship Goal
My Well-Being Goal
My Career Goal
My Leisure Goal
My Hobbies Goal
My Priority Goal is:

Think about your Priority Goal and ask yourself two questions:

1. On a scale of 1 to 10 how much good will come if I achieve this goal and everything turns out well? 1 2 3 4 5 6 7 8 9 10

2. On a scale of 1 to 10 how much will my life be affected if I don't achieve this goal or things do not turn out well? 1 2 3 4 5 6 7 8 9 10

Think about your answers:

- If your answer to 1 is higher than your answer to 2, it is clear you should go for it.

- If your answer to 2 is higher than your answer to 1, think about a different goal.

- If your answers to 1 and 2 are the same, think about how you can increase the upside. Then just do it!

- If you can't think of an upside, don't do anything and think about your goal again tomorrow.

Appendices

Appendix 1
How to help children and young people become more resilient – some top tips for adults

Appendix 2
Information Sheet for Parents & Carers
What is resilience?

Appendix 3
Letter to Parents & Carers

Appendix 1

How to help children and young people become more resilient – some top tips for adults

- Be resilient yourself. Don't pretend you don't have problems - show young people that you are able to cope with uncertainty, changes and difficult times and still get on with enjoying your life.

- Don't try to hide your emotions. Children and young people are much more aware than you think and are likely to know if you are pretending. It is important to be honest about how you feel, and this will show them that expressing your emotions is OK.

- Don't try to protect children and young people from problems and difficulties. Explain to them that making mistakes and coping with tough times are how we grow to be stronger, more capable people.

- When they have a problem, help young people to remember what they have done well in the past or how they were able to solve a problem. Thinking about a past success or achievement can motivate you to find ways to deal with the current problem. You can do this using solution-focused techniques.

- When a child is worried about something, help them to think about what they can do to reduce the worry, and not to focus too much on what they can't do.

- Help children and young people to develop optimistic thinking. Optimistic thinking is about thinking positively, and this can help us overcome difficulties and find solutions to problems.

- Show young people that you care about their friendships. Friendships are very important to children and young people – often more than some adults realise. Try to understand how they feel if they are excited about a new friendship or if a friend lets them down.

- Help young people to make friends with other children and adults. Encourage them to be friendly in order to make friends and to try to really understand other people. The social support that comes from having good relationships is really important for resilience. Relationships also help in developing skills such as communication, co-operation and problem-solving.

- Help young people to realise that not everyone has to like them for them to be a worthwhile person. Popularity is not the most important thing.

- Help them find simple things to do that they really enjoy – things that put a smile on their face. When we feel good our minds become more open to possibilities and solutions.

- Spend time with children and young people to show that you care and are supportive. Don't feel this has to be special free time – often the best way to get to know a child is to work with them on a task like cooking or washing dishes or making something together.

Appendices

- Let young people know that they can trust you by, as far as possible, doing what you say you're going to do.

- Give children and young people tasks to do to help out at home, at school or at a club. This will help them to feel that they can contribute and take responsibility. Give praise for a task well done.

- Help older children develop a sense of responsibility for their own lives. Feelings of responsibility increase confidence, which in turn helps us deal with challenges.

- Give children and young people choices. This will allow them to feel responsible for making decisions for themselves. Even young children like to make choices about what they eat or what toy to play with. Be careful not to give too many options though, as this could be confusing for young children.

- Give young people opportunities to try new things so that they can learn what they really like to do, what they are good at and not so good at.

- Give encouragement and praise when they have done something well or tried hard – this will help them feel more confident and more likely to try again.

- Show young people you care by really listening to them when they talk. Try to really understand where they're coming from.

- Give young people rules that they understand – they respond well to rules and boundaries but they need to be able to make sense of them. Ask them to help set the rules, and agree the consequences of breaking them.

- Create security for younger children by having daily routines and sticking to them – like always having the same bed time. This structure in their lives can be comforting.

- Make sure young people get enough sleep, exercise and healthy food to help them have the energy to cope with life. Teach older children how to look after themselves too.

- Have high, but realistic, expectations of them. Believe in them – every child is unique, worthwhile and has their own unique strengths, such as kindness, curiosity or perseverance.

Appendix 2

Information Sheet for Parents & Carers

What is resilience?

Resilience is about 'bouncing back' from the things that life presents to us. It is about being strong inside and able to adapt well to changes, challenges and difficulties. It is also about 'flourishing' in life, despite our circumstances or the challenges we may face.

How will this benefit my child?

If children are resilient they will be able to cope better with problems, they will have better health and they will be happier and more fulfilled overall. They will also be less likely to develop emotional problems and mental health problems such as depression or anxiety. By supporting the development of their resilience, health and well-being, children can:

- Develop psychologically, emotionally, intellectually and spiritually.
- Initiate, develop and sustain mutually satisfying personal relationships.
- Use and enjoy solitude.
- Become aware of others and empathise with them.
- Play and learn.
- Develop a sense of right and wrong.
- Resolve (and face) problems and setbacks and learn from them.

How will the programme be structured?

'Bouncing Back & Coping with Change' is a 20-session programme. All the sessions will take place as a group or whole class and cover seven different areas of resilience. Within each session, the group are introduced to activities and resources that give each of them the opportunity to think more about what they have learned in school and at home.
The programme will be evaluated, with the young people rating themselves on their ability to bounce back in different situations before and after taking part.

Where can I find out more information?

Please contact the person named on the accompanying letter if you have any queries, concerns or are simply interested in finding out more.

Appendices

Appendix 3

Letter to Parents & Carers

Dear Parents and Carers,

As children grow, it is very important that they develop **resilience** to cope better with the uncertainties and problems that they may face. Research shows that resilience is not just something that people have or do not have, but that there are many ways in which it can be nurtured and enhanced.

Bouncing Back & Coping with Change is the topic of a 20-session programme that will be delivered in school this term. Through child-friendly and fun activities, the programme aims to promote emotional resilience, to develop skills in positive communication and emotional self-regulation and to help our children find ways to be happier and to bounce back from setbacks.

It is a priority of this school that all of our children are able to identify and build upon their strengths across all aspects of their lives. The programme will equip children with a range of skills and strategies which will help them develop the happy habits of positive thinking. We are pleased to enclose an information sheet which will provide more detail about the programme.

We hope you appreciate the importance of this programme for the well-being and emotional resilience of your child and will support them as they progress through the sessions.

Thank you.

If you have any concerns about this programme or require any further information please contact:

References & Bibliography

Baer R.A. (2003) 'Mindfulness training as a clinical intervention: A conceptual and empirical review', *Clinical Psychology: Science and Practice*, 10, 125–43.

Baer R.A. (2006) *Mindfulness-based Treatment Approaches: Clinician's Guide to Evidence Base and Applications*, Burlington: Academic Press.

Baer R.A. & Krietemeyer J. (2006) 'Overview of mindfulness and acceptance based treatment approaches', in R.A. Baer (ed.), *Mindfulness-based Treatment Approaches: Clinician's Guide to Evidence Base and Applications*, Burlington: Academic Press.

Bandura A. (1977) *Social Learning Theory*, Englewood Cliffs, NJ: Prentice Hall.

Block, J., & Kremen, A. M. (1996) 'IQ and ego-resiliency: Conceptual and empirical connections and Separateness', *Journal of Personality and Social Psychology*, 70, 349–61.

Bowlby J. (1969) *Attachment. Attachment and Loss: Vol. 1 Loss*, New York: Basic Books.

Bryant F. B. & Veroff J. (2006) *Savoring: A new model of positive experience*, London: Routledge.

Cairns K. (2002) *Attachment, Trauma and Resilience: Therapeutic Caring for Children*, London: BAAF.

Cameron R. & Maginn C. (2008) 'The authentic warmth dimension of professional childcare', *British Journal of Social Work*, 38(6), 1151–72.

Cox T. (1981) *Stress*, 2nd edn, London: MacMillan.

Craig C. (2007) *Creating Confidence: A Handbook for Professionals Working with Young People*, Glasgow: The Centre for Confidence and Well-being.

Daniel B. & Wassell S. (2002) *Assessing and Promoting Resilience in Vulnerable Children*, Vols 1, 2 & 3, London: Jessica Kingsley Publishers.

Duckworth A., Peterson C., Matthews M.D. & Kelly D.R. (2007) 'Grit: Perseverance and Passion for Long-Term Goals', *Journal of Personality and Social Psychology*, 92(6), 1087–1101.

Dunham J. (1992) *Stress in Teaching*, 2nd edn, London: Routledge.

Evangelou M., Taggart B., Sylva K., Melhuish E., Sammons P. & Siraj-Blatchford I. (2008) *What Makes a Successful Transition from Primary to Secondary School*, London: EPPSE Project, Department for Children, Schools and Families.

Feldman G., Hayes A. & Kumar S. et al. (2007). 'Mindfulness and emotion regulation: The development and initial validation of the cognitive and affective mindfulness scale-revised (CAMS-R)', *Journal of Psychopathology and Behavioral Assessment*, 29(3), 177–90.

Fox-Eades J. (2008) *Celebrating Strengths: Building Strengths-Based Schools*, Coventry: CAPP Press.

Fredrickson B. (2003) 'The value of positive emotions', *American Scientist*, 91, 330–35.

Fredrickson B. (2009) *Positivity – Groundbreaking Research to Release your Inner Optimist and Thrive*, Oxford: One World.

Frydenberg E. (1997) *Adolescent Coping: Theoretical and Research Perspectives*, London: Routledge.

Goodman T.A. (2005) 'Working with children: Beginner's mind', in C.K. Germer, R. D. Segal & P.R. Fulton (eds.), *Mindfulness and psychotherapy*, New York: Guilford Press, 197–219.

Greeson J. M. (2009) 'Mindfulness Research Update 2008', *Complimentary Health Practice Review* 14(1), 10–18.

Hallowell E. (2002) *The Childhood Roots of Adult Happiness*, London: Vermillion.

Hughes F. (2003) 'Spontaneous play in the 21st century', in O. Saracho & B. Spodek (eds), *Contemporary Perspectives on Play in Early Childhood Education*, Greenwich, CT: Information Age Publishing, 21–40.

Huppert F.A. & Johnson D.M. (2010) 'A controlled trial of mindfulness training schools: The importance of practice for an impact on wellbeing', *The Journal of Positive Psychology*, 5(4), 264–74.

James W.(1890) *The Principles of Psychology*, Volume 1, New York: Holt.

Kabat-Zinn J. (1990) *Full Catastrophe Living: Using the Wisdom of Your Body and Mind to Face Stress, Pain and Illness*, New York: Delacorte.

Kabat-Zinn J. (1996) *Full Catastrophe Living: How to Cope with Stress, Pain and Illness Using Mindfulness Meditation*, London: Piatkus Books.

Kabat-Zinn J. (2003) 'Mindfulness-based interventions in context: Past, present and future', *Clinical Psychology: Science and Practice*, 10, 144–56.

Kelly G.A. (1955) *The Psychology of Personal Constructs*, New York: Norton.

Lim K, Corlett L, Thompson L, Law J, Wilson P, Gillberg C. & Minnis H. (2010) 'Measuring attachment in large populations: A systematic review', *Educational and Child Psychology* 27(3), 22–32.

MacConville R.M. (2009) *Teaching Happiness: A Ten Step Curriculum for Creating Positive Classrooms*, London: Optimus Education.

MacConville R.M. (2011) *Building Resilience: A Skills-Based Programme to Support Achievement in Young People*, Milton Keynes: Speechmark Publishing.

MacConville R. & Rae T. (2012) *Building Happiness, Resilience and Motivation in Adolescents: A Positive Psychology Curriculum for Well-being*, London: Jessica Kingsley Publishers.

Marlatt G.A. & Kristeller J.L. (1999), 'Mindfulness and meditation', in W.R. Miller et al (eds) *Integrating spirituality into treatment: Resources for practitioners*, Washington DC, American Psychological Association, 67–84.

Mayle D. (2006) *Managing Innovation and Change*, London: Sage.

McGrath H. & Nobel T. (2003) *Bounce Back! A Classroom Resiliency Programme*, Australia: Pearson Longman.

Millward R., Kennedy E., Towlson K. & Minnis H. (2006) 'Reactive attachment disorder in looked-after children', *Emotional & Behavioural Difficulties*, 11(4), 273–79.

Newman T. (2002) *Promoting Resilience: A Review of Effective Strategies for Child Care Services*, Exeter: University of Exeter Centre for Evidence-Based Social Services.

Newton T. (1995) *Managing Stress: Emotion and Power at Work*, London: Sage.

NHS Health Scotland (2006) *The Warwick-Edinburgh Mental Well-being Scale* (WEMWBS).

Office for National Statistics (2003) *The Mental Health of Young People Looked After by Local Authorities*, London: National Stationery Office.

Perry B. & Hambrick E. (2008) 'The Neurosequential Model of Therapeutics', *Reclaiming Children and Youth*, 17(3), 38–43.

Peterson, C & Seligman, M. (2004). *Character Strengths and Virtues: A Handbook and Classification*. Oxford: Oxford University Press.

Prever M. (2006) *Mental Health in Schools: A Guide to Pastoral and Curriculum Provision*, London: Paul Chapman Publishing.

Rae T. (2010) *Managing Stress: A Comprehensive Programme to Support Young People*, London: Optimus Education.

Rae T. (2012) *Developing Emotional Literacy with Teenagers Building Confidence, Self-Esteem and Self Awareness*, 2nd edn, London: Sage.

Rae T. & Egan S. (2009) *Cognitive Behavioural Approach for Secondary Staff and Students*, London: Optimus Education.

Rae T. & Smith E. (2009) *Motivational Interview Approach for Secondary Staff and Students*, London: Optimus Education.

Rae T. & Smith E. (2009) *Solution Focused Approach for Secondary Staff and Students*, London: Optimus Education.

Reivich K. & Shatte A. (2002) *The Resilience Factor*, New York: Broadway Books.

Rohner R.P. (2004). 'The "parental acceptance–rejection syndrome": Universal correlates of perceived rejection', *American Psychologist*, 59, 830–40.

Roskies E. & Lazarus R. (1980) 'Coping theory and the teaching of coping skills', in D. Davidson & S. Davidson (eds), *Behavioral Medicine: Changing Health Lifestyles*, New York: Brunner/Mazel, 38–69.

Rutter M. (1985) 'Resilience in the face of adversity: protective factors and resistance to psychiatric disorder', *British Journal of Psychiatry*, 147, 598–611.

Rutter M. (1987) 'Psychosocial resilience and protective mechanisms', *American Journal of Orthopsychiatry*, 57(3), 316–31.

Rutter M. (1991) *Childhood Experiences and Adult Psychosocial Functioning*, CIBA Foundation Symposium, 189–200.

Saltzman A. & Goldin P. (2008) 'Mindfulness-Based Stress Reduction for School-Age Children', in L.A. Greco & S.C. Hayes (eds) *Acceptance and Mindfulness Treatments for Children & Adolescents*, Oakland: New Harbinger Publications, 139–61.

Segal Z., Williams J. & Teasdale J. (2002) *Mindfulness-based Cognitive Therapy for Depression: A New Approach to Preventing Relapse*, New York: Guilford Press.

Seligman M. (1995) *The Optimistic Child*, New York: Houghton Mifflin.

Seligman M. (2003) *Authentic Happiness: Using the New Positive Psychology to Realize Your Potential for Lasting Fulfilment*, New York: Free Press.

Seligman M. (2006) *Learned Optimism: How to Change Your Mind and Your Life*, New York: Vintage Books.

Seligman M. (2008) TED Talks, July.

Seligman M. (2011) *Flourish: A New Understanding of Happiness and Well-being and How to Achieve Them*, London: Nicholas Brearley Publishing.

Seligman M. & Csikszentmihalyi M. (2000) 'Positive Psychology: An introduction', *American Psychologist*, 55, 5–14.

Semple R. & Lee J. (2008) 'Treating anxiety with mindfulness: Mindfulness-based cognitive therapy for children', in L.A. Greco & S.C. Hayes (eds) *Acceptance and mindfulness treatments for children and adolescents*, Oakland: New Harbinger Publications, 63–87.

Teicher M., Andersen S., Polcari A., Anderson C., Navalta C. & Kim D. (2003) 'The neurobiological consequences of early stress and childhood maltreatment', *Neuroscience and Biobehavioral Reviews*, 27(1–2), 33–44.

Walker J. (2008) 'The use of attachment theory in adoption and fostering', *Adoption and Fostering*, 32(1), 49–56.